BEOWULF

George Quasha
Department of English
New York University

D0682197

1997 Barnes & Noble Books

MACMILLAN is a registered trademark of Macmillan, Inc.
Monarch and colophons are trademarks of Simon & Schuster, Inc.,
registered in the U.S. Patent and Trademark Office.

Macmillan Publishing USA
A division of Simon & Schuster, Inc.
1633 Broadway
New York, NY 10019

ISBN 0-7607-0560-7

Text design by Tony Meisel

Printed and bound in the United States of America.

99 00 01 M 9 8 7 6 5 4 3

RRDC

CONTENTS

INTRODUCTION
EARLY HISTORY OF ENGLAND

THE ROMANS

Writing in the first quarter of the eighth century, the Anglo-Saxon historian Bede informs us that the first Roman to reach Britain was Julius Caesar. From other sources we know that Caesar invaded Britain twice, in 55 B.C. and again in 54 B.C. The first invasion was little more than a reconnaissance, lasting only about three weeks; the second was an ambitious undertaking, employing large forces. In both enterprises the Romans experienced a heavy loss of ships to the Channel tides, the power of which they had been unaware. They also were discomfited by the mobility of British chariot warfare. On the second invasion—a failure in terms of the forces employed—some alliances were made and hostages taken, but no Roman troops were left behind. Subsequently, Caesar's energies were diverted to Gallic revolt and then to civil war, and thoughts of the possible occupation of Britain were abandoned. Almost a century would elapse before the conquest of Britain under Claudius.

THE CELTS

The inhabitants of Britain were of Celtic extraction, Celtic peoples having migrated into Europe as early as the ninth century B.C. The Britons were related to the Gauls and as such were certainly no strangers to either the Romans or Julius Caesar. Indeed, military operations had been conducted against the Celts by the Romans from the earliest times, and the Celtic peoples inhabiting Northern Italy had helped fill the ranks of the armies of Hannibal during his invasion of the Roman peninsula in 218–203 B.C. As we shall see, the unsubdued Celtic peoples—such as the Picts (who inhabited present-day Scotland) and the Scots (who inhabited present-day Ireland until the third century A.D.)—eventually overran a large part of Roman Britain.

The Roman conquest and occupation of Britain, begun in A.D. 43 by the emperor Claudius, was consolidated in the reign of the emperor Hadrian by the building of Hadrian's Wall in A.D. 121 as a bulwark against the unruly tribes (the Picts and Scots) of Northern Britain. Generally, the failure of Caesar's invasions hints at weaknesses in the Roman Empire that would not become obvious for several centuries. Caesar's failure on the North parallels Roman operations in the East, where the millionaire Crassus was killed in a war with the Parthians—an exhaustive war in an area that would, like Britain, eventually prove to be more troublesome than Imperial Rome cared to admit. From the establishment of Hadrian's Wall in the second century until well into the fourth century, the Britons enjoyed peace and prosperity. The northern invaders had been largely constrained, and it was not until the third century that the Romans needed to build coastal defense against the sea-raiders, the Saxons. Roman writers of this period employ the term Saxon as a generic classification of several seafaring peoples, including the Angles, Saxons, and Jutes. The first mention of the Angles (from which we get the word England) occurs in *Germania,* written in the first century A.D. by the Roman historian Tacitus. Tacitus's reference to the "Anglii" is rather nebulous; he refers to them merely as an "island people."

DECLINE AND INVASION

The time of troubles for Roman Britain may be said to have begun in the middle of the fourth century, when the Roman garrisons were withdrawn for operations against continental barbarians who were beginning to make inroads upon the Empire. Clearly, the Romans did not regard Britain as an integral part of their empire and were willing to sacrifice it, just as lands east of the Rhine were given up centuries earlier when they became too difficult and costly to defend. The fate of the Britons seems to parallel the fate of the Romans to a degree, because both peoples lost the spirit that characterized the Germanic peoples of this period. Indeed, the Roman symptom had been noticed by Tacitus three centuries earlier.

Contrasting the Roman life of "bread and circuses" with the German, Tacitus describes the virtuous and vigorous life enjoyed by the German tribes; he extols their view of the family as the basic unit of society. By demonstrating the advantages of the more stoic or "natural" man, Tacitus was pointing out the dangers that existed for a society devoted to pleasure. Tacitus's moral might have been drawn for the Britons themselves just as easily: Under peaceful centuries of Roman rule and protection, they, too, had become stultified. When the Britons appealed to Rome for aid against their enemies, the emperor Honorius replied that he could not send aid and that they must look after themselves. According to Bede, it was Honorius's observation that the Britons suffered attack because they lacked the spirit to defend themselves.

Hadrian's Wall, the bulwark against the savage tribes of the North, was overwhelmed by a united force of Picts and Scots in 367, and almost all of Britain was overrun. Roman superiority was reestablished briefly by Theodosius two years later, but internal affairs in the Roman Empire—notably power struggles between military commanders—left Britain undefended for long periods of time. When Magnus Maximus, a Roman military commander in Gaul, determined to seize the Western Empire from the Emperor Gratian, he removed almost all Roman troops from Britain in 383. This operation left Hadrian's Wall completely undefended and ended its usefulness as a container of the Picts and Scots. Thereafter, Roman control of the island wavered until the Britons were left entirely to the mercy of the invaders.

THE ANGLO-SAXON PERIOD

Traditions of the invasions of Britain may be grouped into two categories, the Welsh and the English. The best source for the Welsh tradition is *De Excidu et Conquestu Britanniae (On the Invasion and Conquest of Britain),* composed in the middle of the sixth century by Gildas, a teacher and religious figure. Although there are many errors in the work, and its function is chiefly religious rather than historical, it suggests certain facts about which we would otherwise know nothing. *De Excidu* is apparently Bede's source for the account of the earliest Anglo-Saxon invasions of Britain. In *The History of the English Church and Peoples,* Bede relates that Anglo-Saxon contingents were invited by Vortigern—a fifth-century king of the Britons—to help in the defense against the Picts and Scots. After the successful conclusion of a war against them, however, Vortigern found that his allies did not wish to leave, nor could he dislodge them. Eventually, the Britons were able to defeat the mercenaries and, according to Gildas, this victory was followed by a brief period of peace.

This Vortigern is the king to whom Gildas refers as *superbus Tyrannus.* On the whole, Bede's work integrates the work of Gildas, other legends, accounts, and chronicles with time and place; the result is a rather more definite—though possibly not a more accurate—work.

TRADITIONS

English traditions are found in the Old English poem *The Fight at Finnsburg* and also in the so-called *Finn Episode,* contained in *Beowulf.* The general tradition is that King Hnaef of Denmark and his warriors visited Finn, king of Frisia. A band of Finn's men attacked Hnaef and his men in their mead-hall; a five-day fight ensued. During this period none of the Danes fell, and their attackers were about to retire. Here, unfortunately, the poem breaks off. From *Beowulf,* we learn that Hnaef eventually is killed and a temporary peace is concluded between the two groups. The Danes—except for Hengest, their new leader—go home for the winter but later return with reinforcements. In a subsequent battle, Finn is killed.

THE ANGLO-SAXON CHRONICLE

The *Anglo-Saxon Chronicle,* written in Old English and Latin, is an important source for the partial verification of Welsh and

English traditions, but is not absolutely authoritative. In most of Western Europe, yearly diaries, or chronicles, were kept; in them the significant happenings of the year were recorded. These records were uneven, some years being passed by completely or noted by only a sentence, other years treated extensively according to the taste, disposition, or interests of the chronicler. The *Anglo-Saxon Chronicle* is actually a compilation of seven separate chronicles; six are written in Old English, and one is written in a combination of Old English and Latin. There is evidence to suggest that chronicles were being kept in England as early as the eighth century, although the earliest manuscript of the *Anglo-Saxon Chronicle* dates from about 891.

In one of the texts of the *Chronicle,* an account is given under the dates 449–473 of a kingdom established in Kent by Hengest, his brother Horsa, and his son Aesic. This also includes an account of battles against the Welsh and the arrival of other chieftains: "456. In this year Hengest and Aesic fought the Britons at a place called Crayford and slew four companies there. The Britons then gave up Kent and fled in fear to London."

We notice that the *Chronicle* begins with a date. The manuscript probably was first marked off in lines for each year, to be filled in by the chronicler. Since the entry would depend upon the amount of information available to the compiler, many spaces were left blank. After the date would follow the Old English word *Her,* meaning, literally, "at this place in the annals." The process of gradual recording is probably the main reason for the use of an adverb of place rather than time in a book of annals.

The *Chronicle* has value as history and also occasionally as literature. For example, the entry of 755 (written at least as late as 784 and probably inserted in the earlier year's space) gives an account of Cynewulf and Cyneheard (of the latter's murder of the former), and the little story is often called the first short story because of its delicate denouement.

OTHER RECORDS

The English and Welsh traditions, although suggestive of historical facts, have provided little for the historian except sources for speculation and inquiry. Continental sources are largely fragmentary and do little more than suggest the most general historical outline of the Early Anglo-Saxon period. The historian Zosimus records that in the fifth century, the Britons seceded from the Roman Empire, took up arms, and defeated the barbarians. Zosimus's reference for this account is believed to be a work (subsequently lost) written by the Greek historian Olympidorus, who was contemporary with the events. Other references—and they are few in number—are equally indefinite.

ANGLO-SAXON KINGDOMS
AND THE CONCEPT OF COMITATUS

That the Anglo-Saxon invasions were largely successful, however, is not open to dispute: By the beginning of the seventh century, there were almost a dozen separate Anglo-Saxon kingdoms in Southern England alone. As we have noted, it is difficult to be certain of the historical events of this period, perhaps because of the small-scale conditions of the invasions. The account given by Tacitus in his *Germania* sheds light upon the character of the Anglo-Saxon institutions of the period. Although Tacitus wrote several centuries before the German tribes were to invade Britain, his observations (supported by other evidences) seem valid. He informs us that the Germans considered the family the basic unit of their society, were industrious yet warlike, and chose their kings for birth and their generals for merit. Although slavery existed and it was possible for a German to sell or gamble himself into slavery, the social structure was not rigid, and poorer Germans could rise by demonstrating their bravery and valor in battle.

A particular institution noticed by Tacitus is the *comitatus* (his term), by which a youth would attach himself to a strong leader: ". . . such lads attach themselves to men of mature strength and strong valor." This institution is almost the precursor (on a smaller scale) of certain feudal institutions; more important, it forms the basis for the lord-thane relationships that we will observe in *Beowulf.* The obligation of the lord was to provide his retainers with goods and bounty in exchange for their services. It was considered dishonorable for a lord to be outdone in bravery by one of his thanes; it was equally dishonorable for a thane to leave the battlefield upon which his lord remained. In the *Nibelungenlied* we see evidences of this in "comrades of the sword," and in Anglo-Saxon England this tradition would persist until well into the tenth century.

We may see that the numerous chieftains or lords with personal bands of followers would, in a sense, represent no more than "adventurers," and as such would not be at great pains to provide history with a record of their accomplishments or deeds.

CHRISTIANITY
According to Bede, the British king Lucius sent a letter to Eleutherius and asked to become a Christian (A.D. 156). The *Chronicle* gives the date as 167, but in any case it is obvious that many Celts had become Christianized during the Roman occupations. The conversion of the Anglo-Saxons began in 597, when Pope Gregory the Great sent St. Augustine (not to be confused with the St. Augustine who wrote *The City of God*) to England with instructions to proceed slowly in his conversion of the Anglo-Saxons. The institutions of the English were to be slowly and patiently transformed, a distinct contrast to the manner that Charlemagne, "Knight of the Christian Faith," later would employ when he gave his subjects the choice of Christianity or the sword. This deliberate policy suggested by Pope Gregory goes far in explaining

the late persistence of Germanic traditions in Britain; as we shall see later, it also accounts for mixtures of pagan and Christian elements in *Beowulf* and other Old English literature.

After Augustine converted Kent, Canterbury became the center of Roman Church activity in Britain early in the seventh century. The Synod of Whitby in 661 marked the first step in the gradual ascendancy of the Roman Church in England; and although there was some backsliding toward heathenism or heterodoxy, the influence of the church gradually extended itself. Canterbury, York, and other monasteries became centers of learning and of Latin and Greek scholarship. As we might remember from later English history, the geography of Britain—that is, its insularity—tended to permit the English a life less subject to papal control than that of their continental neighbors.

ARCHAEOLOGICAL EVIDENCE

While coins and inscriptions and dwelling sites constitute most of the body of remnants of Romano-British civilization, there is little similar evidence of Anglo-Saxon civilization. Since the Anglo-Saxons built their houses of wood, left few inscriptions, and did not manufacture their own coins, there is little left to the archaeologist but objects left in the graves of the dead. Generally, the Anglo-Saxons buried their dead in shallow graves and did not mark them by any special mound or means. However, the pattern of the already uncovered graves indicates (because of their sparseness in the North) that the Anglo-Saxon conquest of Northern England was little more than an imposition of rule upon a basic Celtic population (as opposed to Southern England, which the Anglo-Saxons inhabited extensively).

PLACE-NAMES

Like archaeological evidence left by the Anglo-Saxons, the evidence of place-names is not such that it may easily be assigned a chronology. When a place-name is mentioned by Bede, however, we know that it is at least as old as the eighth century, and scholars may infer that it is much older. Generally, place-names in Britain have remained the same (though there are significant exceptions), except in the cases where a new language and consequently new names have been introduced through invasion. One of the most important of the types of place-names are names that end in *ingas*. This suffix means "follower of," and it usually is combined with a personal name. As an example, Hastings, derived from the Old English, is interpreted as "the followers of Haesta." This name originally applied to a group of people who might be spread over a very large area, pointing to a time in English history when the groups of settlers were more important than where they lived. Significantly, place-names are more numerous in areas that lie off the main routes of communication—areas less influenced by external conditions. Thus, a certain conservativism would be evidenced by place-names.

ANGLO-SAXON CULTURE
The Anglo-Saxons, like their Germanic forebears mentioned in Tacitus's *Germania,* probably lived in a tribal state for some time after they arrived in Britain. Originally, the tribe-structure of Anglo-Saxon society was the development of an extremely integrated clan-structure. The tribe had only two classes: the aristocracy (or earls), who claimed descent from a founder of the tribe; and the plebeians and proletarians (or churls), who claimed no such descent and included bondsmen and captives. In addition there were a few men of exception, called freemen, whose status was uncertain and who held this distinction, apparently, as some sort of reward or special favor.

The head of the tribe was the hereditary king; his genealogy was commonly traced from Woden, king of the gods. To advise the king there was a council of elders, the *witan.* This institution persisted late in Britain under the name *witanagemot;* a few modern historians have traced the British parliament back to it. The condensation of power of the *witan* steadily grew during the half-millennium before the year 1000; the power of the aristocracy waxed and waned in long cycles; and the power of the Anglo-Saxon kings was chiefly dependent upon the residual principle—that is, if the king did not possess the ability to take advantage of the power condensation, it went elsewhere.

The importance of the individual in Anglo-Saxon society was a direct function of social class. As we shall see in *Beowulf,* the vendetta or revenge motive was perfectly acceptable as a means of "law." In the transition from the law of vendetta to the rule of law, however, the *wergild* or blood-money is an interesting example. The law of the *wergild* specified that a person who had suffered damages through the killing of a relative might exact a sum of money from the murderer as an expiation of the crime. The value of an earl was assessed higher than a freeman; a freeman was assessed higher than a churl. Within a class, men were assessed higher than women.

The assessment of women for *wergild* suggests that the Anglo-Saxons valued women less than men. In *Beowulf,* in fact, only one female character assumes any sort of life at all: Wealhtheow, Hrothgar's wife. The Anglo-Saxon woman was expected to be domestic and moral. She was, however, accorded her full legal rights and a certain respect that approached idealization. From *Beowulf* we also learn that it was the function of some aristocratic women to act as peacemakers or arbitrators.

From the literature of the period—and as we shall see in *Beowulf*—there are very few glimpses of the daily life of the so-called average person. The coast-guardsman represents the most ordinary character we shall meet in *Beowulf.* Little is made of him, his life, or preferences; only his function is important. Like the television dramas of today, Old English literature presents on a superficial level too little of the Anglo-Saxon's occupations and hopes, and perhaps too much of hating and violence. Between the deserts of humanity's grim struggle, however, stand a few oases of morality and aspiration. *Beowulf* provides a better view of hope and a more positive preoccupation with the meaning of life than do, for example, *The Fight at Finnsburg* and *The Battle of Brunanburh*.

SUTTON HOO

In 1939 at a private estate in southeastern Suffolk, the remains of a ship-burial that occurred sometime in the middle of the seventh century were uncovered. The name of the estate is Sutton Hoo burial-ship. Although this was not the first burial-ship to be discovered by archaeologists, it was a remarkable find because of the richness in cultural and material objects found at the site.

The burial-ship had never been to sea, perhaps; rather, it may have reflected an old Scandinavian custom of setting the dead hero or king afloat, surrounded with treasure. This was based upon the notion that the dead were undertaking a journey during which (or at the end of which) they would require the treasure and belongings accompanying them. The "journeying of the dead" is a notion common to many mythologies, and we remember the Egyptian bark of the dead as well as Charon's Ferry across the Styx in Greek mythology.

It seems likely that the Sutton Hoo burial-ship served as a cenotaph or memorial to some Anglo-Saxon king who was buried elsewhere. Scholars consider that the king may be identified either as the East Anglian King Anna (died 654) or as Aethelhere (died 655). This would date the burial-ship at a point in time less than one century earlier than the composition of *Beowulf*. For this reason, then, the Sutton Hoo discovery deserves our attention.

The effects found in the burial-ship show clearly that the Anglo-

Saxons had developed a sophisticated culture. The workmanship of the gold objects found is of a very high degree; other objects, such as a small harp, signify that music and poetry held a favored position in the court life of the times. In addition there are many items of solid gold and silver, gold and silver coins (which were useful in determining the date of the burial), and other objects that imply a high level of material wealth. The presence of Christian objects (and the absence of a body) imply that the pagan customs were rapidly being superseded by Christian beliefs.

Before the discovery of Sutton Hoo, the account of the funeral of Scyld Sceafing in *Beowulf* was considered merely a romantic flight of the poet's imagination. The interpretation given to Anglo-Saxon society tended to emphasize the primitiveness and coarseness of it (regarding the Anglo-Saxons as having progressed no further than Tacitus's Germans), but today we see that this interpretation was erroneous. *Voyage to the Other World: The Legacy of Sutton Hoo,* edited by Calvin B. Kendall and Peter S. Wells (Minneapolis, 1992), offers essays about the burial-ship; *The Age of Sutton Hoo: The Seventh Century in North-Western Europe,* edited by M. O. H. Carver (Rochester, NY, 1992), contains many photographs of it.

The significance of Sutton Hoo in our study of Old English literature is very great and has not been exhausted by scholars. Prof. Bessinger has explored the significance of the harp in relation to poetry. (See Bibliography for his article and his impressive recording of Caedmon's *Hymn* with the harp.) Prof. Wrenn has examined the aspects of the Sutton Hoo evidence as regards *Beowulf.* (See Critical Commentary.)

THE ENGLISH LANGUAGE

INTRODUCTION
It is acceptable to refer to the literature that we are about to examine as either Old English or Anglo-Saxon. Academically, "Old English" is preferred, for it implies a continuity of the language and literature of England from the earliest to the present times. As we have seen, the word "England" is derived from "Angle-land," although Anglo-Saxon writers who wrote in Latin referred to their language as *Lingua Anglica* or *Lingua Saxonica*. Alfred the Great, writing in the ninth century, referred to his language as *Englisc*.

THE ANGLO-SAXON LANGUAGE
Old English, a term that refers to the language of both the Angles and the Saxons (since it was the same), persisted as a written means of expression for some time after the spoken word had developed from Old to Middle English late in the eleventh and in the beginning of the twelfth centuries. Historically, English is a derivative of the ancestral Indo-European language (also called Indo-Germanic), which probably was spoken before recorded history around Lithuania and southern Russia. The language divided into nine groups (probably as early as 2500 B.C.): Indian, Iranian, Armenian, Hellenic, Albanian, Italic, Balto-Slavic, Germanic (Teutonic), and Celtic. Each of these groups subdivided into the languages that we know as the moderns. The Teutonic branch divided into East Teutonic, North Teutonic, and West Teutonic.

DIVISIONS OF OLD ENGLISH
Generally Old English is divided into two periods: (1) Early Old English—from A.D. 700 to 900; and (2) Late Old English—from A.D. 900 to about 1100. In our study of Old English language and literature, we are concerned almost exclusively with Late Old English, for the only reliable document we have from the Early Old English is King Alfred's translation of *Cura Pastoralis*. Even this document, from late in the Early English

period, shows that the language is transitional to Late Old English. Classical Old English, therefore, is the Late Old English of Aelfric in prose and *Beowulf* in poetry. Some texts were written earlier, but the form in which they presently exist is that of a scribe's version of the Late Old English period, usually from around the year A.D. 1000. (The student should keep in mind that dates assigned to manuscripts are constantly being debated by scholars, for linguistic, literary, cultural, and archeological evidence must be weighed and compared before even an approximate date of composition can be agreed upon.)

CLASSICAL OLD ENGLISH

The center of Late Old English, or the classical language in which *Beowulf* is written, is that of King Alfred the Great in the southern and southwestern region of Wessex (West Saxon). Modern English is not actually derived specifically from this language but from the East Midland (Anglian) dialect of King Offa the Mercian. (It is easy to see that the term Old English, while justly indicating the continuity of the literature, is something of a misnomer in terms of linguistics.) At this time there were four major dialects: (1) West Saxon: the Saxon dialect of the Wessex kingdom (for the other dialects produced no writing that remains); (2) Kentish: Southeastern England; (3) Mercian: West Midland, from which Modern English derives; and (4) Northumbrian. Most grammars take the language of Aelfric as the authority.

It is interesting to note that the Celtic language continued to be spoken throughout the Anglo-Saxon period in the more remote parts of Britain. Another language, Old Norse, appeared in the latter half of the ninth century, brought over by Viking raiders. This language also persisted for a few centuries, but neither language—Celtic or Old Norse—was so sufficiently general as to make its effects felt in the literature.

THE ALPHABET

In Beowulf it will be seen that Hrothgar is able to read runes that are inscribed upon the hilt of a sword presented him as a trophy. The runic alphabet was introduced into Britain by the Anglo-Saxons themselves, and it enjoyed a somewhat limited popularity. The Latin alphabet, which was capable of rendering most Old English sounds, was used, generally, and with only slight modification. Runic inscriptions, however, have been found and dated as early as the fourth century A.D. in Denmark. The same series of runes came into use in Western Germany perhaps a century and a half later. Scholars have suggested that the runic alphabet was derived from a North Italic alphabet by the Eruli, a people who inhabited Denmark from the middle of the fifth century A.D. Without going too deeply into the development of the runes, the "English" Runic Alphabet progressed geographically from Scandinavia along the coast of the North Sea and was then brought to England by the Anglo-Saxons. These runes are called Anglo-Frisian and are found on twoscore or so inscriptions on coins, burial objects, and so on. In addition there are a few stones bearing runes in the north of England. The last English runic inscriptions belong to the tenth century, and they seem not to have been used much for monuments after the Danish invasion in 865. The decline of the runic alphabet, of course, coincided with the rise of the Latin alphabet.

The student of Old English needs to be familiar with only a few fundamentals before beginning to decipher the original texts. (For those interested, it is possible to begin reading almost immediately with the aid of a translation. Below we will have occasion to compare a few lines of Old and Modern English.) For example, the thorn sign þ stood for a vowel sound equal to that in our *that* or *than*. The different *th* sounds of *then* and *thin,* while originally differentiated, came to be represented interchangeably by the thorns þ and ð. (Wherever the student reads *th* in the following Old English poetry, a thorn appeared originally!) The Old English *y* was pronounced like the German *u*—a sound that has passed out of modern English.

THE LORD'S PRAYER: TWO VERSIONS

Some of the differences and similarities become apparent in a comparison of two texts of the Lord's Prayer (Matthew 6:9–13), one being found in Old English versions and the other being the more familiar one found in the King James (Authorized) Version of the Bible.

Faeder ure *th*u *th*e eart on heofonum si *th*in nama gehalgod. Tobecume *th*in rice. Gewur*th*e *th*in willa on eor*th*an swa swa on heofonum. Urne gedaeghwamlican hlaf syle us to daeg. And forgyf us ure gyltas swa swa we forgyfa*th* urum gyltendum. And ne gelaed *th*u us on costnunge ac alys us of yfele. So*th*lice.

Our father which art in heaven, hallowed be thy name. Thy kingdom come. Thy will be done in earth, as it is in heaven. Give us this day our daily bread. And forgive us our debts, as we forgive our debtors. And lead us not into temptation, but deliver us from evil . . . Amen.

We can see immediately that Modern English has become quite a different language. This development, as we shall see, is the result of a complex process of linguistic influences. In the above we also notice that the changes are largely orthographic (in spelling). *Hlaf,* for example, has become *loaf*—the *h* is dropped and the vowel changed. *Faeder* is *father.* On the other hand, some words have been replaced, as with the change from *costnung* (seen here in the dative case, *costnunge*) to the French importation *temptation.*

Grammatically, Old English differed quite a bit from Modern English. It was (like Latin, Greek, and Modern German as well as Russian) a more highly inflected language; that is, among other things, its nouns took case endings, its verbs took more person and number endings, its adjectives took endings, and so on. There were four cases of nouns: nominative, genitive, dative, and accusative. Adjectives took the same ending plus the instrumental case. (We remember that modern English has only two cases for nouns, including the possessive, and none for adjectives.) For example, *heofonum* (heaven), used above, is the dative singular (object of the preposition on, meaning in). *Forgyfath* (forgive) is the first-person plural of the verb.

Grammatical relationships were expressed by the special endings. In Modern English, grammatical relationships are expressed by a much more rigid syntax or word order than Old English required. Thus, in Old English poetry, word order could be altered severely to meet metrical requirements. An example of the differences can be seen in the following: *urne gedaeghwamlican hlaf syle us* is reversed in Modern English *Give us our daily bread.*

VOCABULARY DIFFERENCES

Old English, like all languages, borrowed words from foreign languages; it borrowed from Latin and Norse, for example. But basically it was unilingual in that it formed new words by compounds made up of its own roots. Note the following process: *mod*—heart or spirit or mind (which became Modern English *mood*); *modig*—spirited, by addition of *ig* (roughly equivalent to *y* in adjective endings; so *blodig*, for example, means bloody); *modcraeft*—intelligence, by addition of *craeft,* meaning "skill" or "craft"; thus it means literally "skill of mind"; *unmod*—depression, by addition of the prefix *un; guthmodig*—of warlike mind or warlike, by addition of guth, meaning war.

The fact that the majority of Old English words were of native origin is perhaps the greatest difference between that language and Modern English. Only about fourteen percent of the words in *Webster's New World Dictionary* have been derived from Old English. Of course, many of the frequently used words are those from Anglo-Saxon—words like *I, the, and, man, woman,* and *loaf.* In fact, more than 60 percent of most frequently used thousand words in our speaking vocabularies are derived from Old English.

THE DEVELOPMENT OF MODERN ENGLISH

The periods of the development of the English language are generally stated as follows: Old English or Anglo-Saxon—449 to 1066; Middle English—1066 to 1485; Modern English—1485 to present day. These are only convenient dates, for the development of a language is slow and complex. Here, however, are the significant dates regarding this development.

43 to 499: The Romans occupied the island of Britain. They civilized and Christianized many of the Celts who lived there. After the withdrawal of the Romans (for the Empire, under attacks of the barbarians, needed its armies), tribes from the northern coast of Europe invaded. They spoke dialects of Low West Germanic, were pagans, and were much less civilized than the Romans. We group them as the Angles (to the east and north of the island), the Saxons (to the south and west), and the Jutes (in the southeast).

499: This is the date usually assigned to the original Anglo-Saxon invasions. The Roman occupation left relatively little impact on the language of the island. The invading tribes defeated the Celts, fought among themselves, formed independent kingdoms, began to form diplomatic relationships, and were converted to Christianity. Records show that they began to write their language sometime in the seventh century. The influence of Christianity was vital to the course of development the peoples of the island were to take. In 664 the Synod of Whitby resolved many of the differences between the religious positions of the North and the South, of the Irish leadership and that of Rome. Due largely to the influence of Christianity, the language was written by the clerics in monasteries. After the death of Alfred the Great (849–899), the island was overrun by Danes and Norwegians. In 1017 Canute (Cnut), who was to become King of Denmark, held the English throne. But the sturdy English culture prevailed. The last Anglo-Saxon king was Edward the Confessor (1041–1066)

1066: This is the date of the Norman Conquest, led by Duke William. For several hundred years after this, the kings of England spoke French as their first language. French became the aristocratic language and it profoundly influenced the course of Middle and Modern English. A great change took place in the language after this. More than ten thousand French words were introduced into the language, particularly in the areas most in the hands of the aristocracy—law, government, the military, art, and medicine. Some French words (as we saw above with *temptation* in place of *costnung*) took the place of the Old English. Often Old English, French, and Latin words took on subtleties of difference, as in *holy, sacred,* and *consecrated*. But by the time of Chaucer (1340–1400), English had become the language of literature and society. As in Old English, there were several major dialects, but East Midland became preeminent for several reasons: it was spoken in London; it was used by William Caxton, the first English printer, when he set up his press in 1476; and it was Chaucer's language. But some major literature was written in other dialects: for example, *Piers Plowman, Sir Gawain and the Green Knight,* and *Pearl*.

1485: This is the date of the accession to the English throne of Henry VII, the first of the Tudors, and it is a convenient date for the beginning of Modern English. Of course, Modern English is not one language and has itself gone through a complex process of development. It is sometimes divided as follows: Early Modern English—1485 to 1700; Late Modern English—after 1700.

Early Modern English, the language of the sixteenth and seventeenth centuries, is not by any means the language we speak today, but it is familiar to us because it is the language of the King James Version of the Bible (quoted above) and of Shakespeare. Pronunciation and usage have changed a great deal since then, and even the best of today's actors would not have been understood by Shakespeare's audience. Late Modern English came with the eighteenth century and attempts to formalize the language. In 1603 the first English dictionary had been published, but the age of dictionaries followed the publication in 1755 of Samuel Johnson's *English Dictionary*. The spirit of the sixteenth and seventeenth century had been one of adventure and seeking to discover new realms—hence Sharespeare's "explosion" of the language into new words and ways of writing. In the neoclassical eighteenth century, the direction was toward the formal. Academicians sought to find a grammar for a language which was thought to be undignified without it. American English is the latest major development of Late Modern English, and, as H. L. Mencken never tired of pointing out, it represents a renaissance of its own kind. The American language is somewhat in the position of sixteenth-century English in that it is in the process of existing without strong rules. Unlike the language of *Beowulf,* it borrows from everywhere; like the language of Shakespeare, it is relatively new and lends itself to new forms.

A FINAL GLIMPSE OF DIFFERENCES

The above summary provides some perspective on the development of the language of *Beowulf* into the complex group of dialects, called English, which is spoken natively by over a quarter of a billion people (and by millions more as a second language). The final sequence should make the process clearer. The following are eight translations of one verse from the Bible, Matthew 5:13:

Old English, 995
Ge synd eor*th*an sealt; gyf *th*aet sealt awyr*th*, on *th*am *th*e hit

gesylt bi*th*? (Literal translation: you are the earth salt; if the salt away—does, with what that it salted is [will be]?)

Wycliffe Gospels, 1389
Yee ben salt of the erthe; that yif the salt shal vanyshe away, wherynne shal it be saltid?

Tyndale Gospels, 1526
Ye are the salt of the erthe; but and if the salt be once vnsavery, what can be salted ther with?

Geneva Bible, 1560
Ye are the salte of the earth: but if the salte haue lost its sauour, wherewith shal it be salted?

Reims (Douai) Bible, 1582
You are the salt of the earth. But if the salt leese his vertue, vvherevvith shall it be salted?

King James, 1611
Yee are the salt of the earth: But if the salt haue lost his sauour, wherewith shal it be salted?

Moffatt Translation, 1922
You are the salt of the earth. But if the salt becomes insipid, what can make it salt again?

Revised Standard, 1952
You are the salt of the earth; but if the salt has lost its taste, how shall its saltness be restored?

The differences are striking, and they illustrate something of the way the language developed. Chaucer wrote a different language, too, but a small lexicon is all we need to understand him. *Beowulf* is another story—and another language. But, in a very real sense, we are not truly reading *Beowulf* if we do not read Old English.

THE ELEMENTS OF ANGLO-SAXON POETRY

PLACE IN THE HISTORY OF POETRY

We saw above that Modern English descends from a dialect other than the one we read in Old English literature. The term "Old English" therefore serves mainly to establish the continuity of the literature, rather than the language. Prof. C. L. Wrenn (see Bibliography) has shown that there has been a continuity in English literature of the Anglo-Saxon tradition in thought, mood, and subject matter and that, on a technical level, Anglo-Saxon meters (syllabic and stress patterns) have persisted. A student of modern poetry knows of the emphasis that certain poets (notably Ezra Pound: see, for example, his translation of *The Seafarer*) have placed on Anglo-Saxon rhythms and subject matter. And one need only listen well to a good reading of Anglo-Saxon poems (such as that by Bessinger on record: see Bibliography) to hear a poetic sensibility—a poetic "ear"—that lives on in the poetry of Gerard Manley Hopkins, James Joyce (especially in *Ulysses* and *Finnegans Wake*), Dylan Thomas, T. S. Eliot (especially in *The Wasteland*), Ezra Pound and others. All of this is by way of saying that Anglo-Saxon is only a "dead" language in the sense that it is not spoken and a "dead" literature in that very few people can read it well enough to realize its rich literary values. Obviously a translation can bring us only the broad outlines of the original and none of the complex nuances of sound and color. As the English poet Coleridge remarked, poetry is that which is lost in translation. (Note: For an example of a close reading of an Anglo-Saxon lyric poem, see the discussion of *The Wanderer* below.)

THE SCOP

Our earliest literatures in virtually all languages are the product of oral traditions that developed out of the first songs sung and tales told. In the case of Anglo-Saxon literature, these traditions go back to the Germanic tribes that lived on the Continent. The poet was a wandering person, like the Provençal troubadour, the German minnesinger, and the French trouvère, minstrel, and jongleur of the Middle Ages, who went to various courts in search of a patron among the lords. The role of the poet, called a scop (which means, literally, a "shaper"), was to entertain during celebrations—feasts involving members of the court—and sing heroic tales. Some of the heroes were real and some legendary, but if their names lived on it was largely because they were the subject of the scop. We will see in *Beowulf* the scop who sings at Hrothgar's court of Sigemund (the Volsung) and his heroic defeat of a dragon. But, as we have seen in our glimpse of the Anglo-Saxon people and language, Christianity had a profound influence upon the traditions that came to be expressed in poetry and prose. Thus the Christian scribes turned their attention to what could in some way fit into Christian ideas, and, since all our manuscripts date from about the year 1000, the subject matter of the scop tends away from pagan conceptions of the heroic to the adapted Christian versions.

THE STRUCTURE OF OLD ENGLISH POETRY

The most striking difference between Old and later English poetry is in its technical structure. Every "line" actually consists of two clearly separated half-lines, between which is a pause (called a caesura). The two parts are united by alliteration—which is really a form of rhyme, an initial rhyme or "head rhyme." Alliteration is conventionally the repetition of consonant sounds, usually at the beginnings of words. However, alliteration or initial rhyme is interpreted in Old English poetry more broadly than has been the case in later literature because, in addition to the repetition of similar consonants, it includes the rhyming of any vowel with any other vowel. (Another instance of the continuity of English poetry is the practice of some modern poets to rely heavily upon such vowel-rhymes within the line as a way of enriching the particular music of the poem.) Every half-line consists of two "feet"—rhythmic stresses or accents. This "foot" is the basic unit of the poetry. The half-line of two feet has its own metrical pattern (and consequently its own scansion or analysis of the metrical pattern, as we shall see below). There is rarely any end-rhyme in Old English poetry, for the practice of rhyming the final words in the lines was a late development in English poetry. (Once again we should note that modern poetry, like Old English poetry, is often organized by methods other than end-rhyme, notably sound devices occurring within the line.) Generally there are three alliterations per line: two in the first half-line and one on the first "foot" of the second half-line. The stressed syllable in the half-line carries the alliteration, and usually the third accented syllable sets up the alliteration. Lines four and five of Beowulf offer a classic example of this alliterative verse:

> Oft S*c*yld S*c*eafing /   s*c*ea*th*ena *th*reatum,
> *m*onegum *m*aed*th*um /   *m*eodosetla ofteah.

> (Oft Scyld Scef's son /   from bands of robbers,
> from many tribes, /   their mead-benches dragged
>   away.)

The italicized sounds alliterate—two in the first half-line and one in the second half-line. There are many variations within the rigidly established pattern, but we cannot fruitfully consider them here. It will be worthwhile to glance at the first lines of *The Seafarer*, the Old English elegy known widely in Ezra Pound's version. We include Pound's version, which captures a good deal of the special music of the Old English but which is at considerable variance from the original in meaning:

> Maeg ic be me sylfum   so*th*gied wrecan,
> si*th*as secgan,   hu ic geswincdagum
> earfo*th*hwile   oft *th*rowade,
> bitre breostceare   gebiden haebbe,
> gecunnad in ceole   cearselda fela,

atol y*th*a gewealc;   *th*aer mec oft bigeat
nearo nihtwaco   aet nacan stefnan,
*th*onne he be clifum cnossa*th* . . .

Pound's version:

> May I for my own self song's truth reckon,
> Journey's jargon, how I in harsh days
> Hardship endured oft.
> Bitter breast-cares have I abided,
> Known on my keel many a care's hold,
> And dire sea-surge, and there I oft spent
> Narrow nightwatch nigh; the ship's head
> While she tossed close to cliffs . . .

We feel in this the rush of the famous "word-horde"—a kenning for poem—the heavy pounding rhythm (appropriate for the subject of severe woes and a rugged existence), the strong alliteration. We feel the force of the seafarer's plight, and his song's musical qualities take us into the experience.

THE KENNING

In addition to the above devices, the scop used a kind of figurative language—the kenning—to embellish ordinary objects. Like the Homeric epithet (such as "swift-footed Achilles" and "rosy-fingered dawn"), the kenning was a standard phrase or metaphor composed of a compound of two words, which became the formula for a specific object: "the leavings of hammers" for swords, the "world-candle" for the sun, "the whale-road" or "sea-monster's home" for the sea, and so on. Very often the lesser poet would resort to kennings that had become clichés, such as using "ring-giver" to describe every prince. But the kenning, used with originality, served the purpose of metaphor, and, like metaphor, its use was varied and complex.

RHETORICAL TECHNIQUES

Rhetorical techniques are those which alter the particular arrangement of words in order to gain special emphasis. They differ from figurative devices like metaphors and kennings in that they do not change the basic meanings of the words used. Thus litotes (a type of meiosis or understatement in which something is stated as less important than it really is) expresses an idea by denying its opposite. These rhetorical techniques are a form of ironic understatement, meant to draw attention to the object. Litotes was a favorite technique by which Old English poetry embellished its subjects. For example, in *Beowulf* the poet describes the end of Grendel's bloody career with these words: "Very different his (Grendel's) fate from that which befell him in earlier days!" In the midst of a grim description of the battle between Beowulf and Grendel, this ironic understatement is an effective device. The poet often elaborated his subject, letting words grow with his awareness of the experience. Again in the Pound translation cited above: "Bitter breast cares have I abided, / Known on my keel many a care's hold . . ." Much world poetry that arises from the oral tradition tends to employ such elaboration as this and tends to make catalogues of the qualities of individuals. For example, Wiglaf is introduced in Canto XXXVI of *Beowulf* as follows: "Wiglaf was called Weohstan's son, / a beloved shield-warrior, a Scylfings' lord, / Aelfhere's kinsman . . ." This piling up of qualities, each of which is a slight variation on the other, is one of the most common rhetorical techniques. We see such variation in the announcement of Beowulf's death in Canto XXXIX:

> Now is the kind giver   of the Weder's people,
> the Goth's lord,   fast on his deathbed.
> He rests on his deadly couch   by the worm's
>   deeds . . .

This is restatement for the poetic purpose of establishing the emotional weight of the death.

OTHER TECHNIQUES

We could mention many other techniques, but we shall confine ourselves to suggesting a couple of others. Envelope pattern is a method of organizing a section of a poem (or whole poem) by beginning and ending it with similar statements and rhythms. Thus lines 74 to 110 in *The Wanderer* form an envelope by beginning with *ealre thisse worulde wela westa stondeth* ("all the wealth of this world will stand waste") and ending with *eal this eorthan gesteal idel weortheth* ("the whole state of the world is vain"). The echoes of sound and general meaning allow a figure-like restatement-variation within which there is a dramatic development of related themes. Generative composition, as defined by Rosier (see Bibliography) is "the reuse within a few lines of a given word which is usually in the same class (viz., noun, adjective, etc.) as the original use, and which may or may not have precisely the same meaning or referent." He distinguished between lexical generation, wherein the word itself influences the choice of words that follow, and conceptual generation, where it is the "idea of a word rather than the word itself which attracts or induces other words . . ." For example, Rosier demonstrates that in *The Wanderer,* which shows the mind of the wanderer as it develops, the words for the mind and its faculties occur throughout the poem—about thirty-five times in 115 lines. (*Mod,* the word for "mind," occurs eight times either alone or in a combination.) It is interesting to reflect upon this kind of composition, for it seems to imply that the poet's sensibility attained its focus literally through words. Rosier cogently argues for this method as a basic organizing device in *The Wanderer,* and it has been shown that much of this occurs in *Beowulf.*

THE BASIS FOR VERSIFICATION

We saw above that the harp found at Sutton Hoo was an important part of the scop's performance. There has been a great deal of speculation about the role of this instrument in Old English versification. An older theory held that the scop struck his harp at each of the four stresses in the line of poetry. It has been suggested more recently, however, that the rests often occurring before unaccented syllables probably took the stroke of the harp. To hear a brilliant hypothetical re-creation of an Old English poem according to this latter theory, the student should listen to Prof. Bessinger's record of readings (see Bibliography), where he plays the Sutton Hoo type of harp while singing Caedmon's *Hymn*.

THE MANUSCRIPTS OF OLD ENGLISH POETRY

As we have said, most of the Old English poetry in existence—a small remnant—comes to us in manuscripts dating from about the year 1000 and written in West Saxon Old English. Many of the originals were written quite a bit earlier, but there is much controversy over the dates. The following are the four principal manuscripts:

1. The *Beowulf* manuscript contains *Beowulf* and *Judith* (the fragment of a religious poem on the Biblical tale: c. ninth century); it is in the Cotton collection of the British Museum.

2. The Junius manuscript contains the Caedmonian poems (religious poems associated with the poet Caedmon, though not written by him; the only poem attributed to Caedmon, the shepherd who was divinely inspired, is the *Hymn,* found in the Latin manuscripts of Bede's *History;* this poem apparently dates from before 737—the date of the poem found in the original Northumbrian dialect); it is in the Bodleian Library at Oxford.

3. The Exeter Book contains *Widsith* (see below), riddles, some Cynewulfian poems (religious poems by or ascribed to the poet Cynewulf—the only Old English poet to have signed any manuscript), and elegies (discussed below); it is in Exeter Cathedral.

4. The Vercelli manuscript contains *Andreas* and *A Dream of the Rood* (the former, a religious poem possibly imitative of *Beowulf;* the latter, a religious lyric and one of the great poems of English literature); it is in Vercelli, in Piedmont, Northern Italy.

HEROIC LITERATURE AND EPICS

THE EPIC

The word "epic" comes from the Greek and means "tale." It is a long narrative poem that deals with themes and characters of heroic proportions. Its style is exalted. We may conveniently divide epics into the two types distinguished by C. S. Lewis. Primary epics are the earliest written versions of poems that, at least in part, came out of an oral tradition. Probably the tales were sung by generations of poets and were finally put into written form by a literate poet or a scribe. The greatest primary epics known to us are the *Iliad,* the *Odyssey,* and *Beowulf.* Secondary epics are later versions that draw some degree of their style and subject matter from earlier epics. In this class we may include Virgil's *Aeneid,* which took its inspiration from Homer. Other works that take their direction at least in part from epics include Dante's *Divine Comedy,* Tasso's *Gerusalema Liberata,* Spenser's *Faerie Queene,* and Milton's *Paradise Lost.*

The conventions of the epic, as established by Homer and Virgil (who, though later than Homer, had a greater influence on literature before the eighteenth century), include an exalted dignified style; a complex theme and narrative that recapitulate the significant preoccupations and experiences of an epoch; a hero who is the epitome of a nation and culture; and a beginning of the narrative in medias res, in the middle of things. There are many other conventions that are too complex to discuss here.

BEOWULF AS EPIC

Beowulf embodies these general characteristics in its own special way. The poet concentrates on a section of the life and exploits of a central hero as part of the historical progression of a people, the ideals of which the hero embodies. Similarly, the focus of the *Iliad* is upon Achilles and certain actions during the Trojan War, the *Odyssey* upon Odysseus and his journey, and the *Aeneid* upon Aeneas. We do not enter in medias res in the sense of the *Iliad*, but we enter Beowulf's life at a particular time and hear of the historical context into which it fits: Scyld Sceafing and the Scyldings, the struggle between the Danes and the Heathobards, and so on. The poem represents the essential elements of the culture in its fusing of pagan and Christian elements. It tells of heroic struggles. And the style is elaborate and exalted in a way that embodies the spirit of its heroic subject.

EARLIER EPICS

Beowulf (c. 650–750) is a relatively late product of Anglo-Saxon civilization, though stylistically, some critics have argued, it represents an earlier stage in the development of oral poetry than do the *Iliad* and the *Odyssey*. There is some possibility that *Beowulf* was indebted to Virgil, since it embodies many of the characteristics of that poet's work. In any case, it is probable that there were fully developed epics in Anglo-Saxon before *Beowulf*, some of which may never have been recorded and others of which may have been lost. The qualities of the earliest epics, products of the oral traditions of the so-called heroic age of the continental Germanic tribes, can perhaps be glimpsed in certain poems and poetic fragments. Among these are *Widsith, Waldere,* and *The Fight at Finnsburg*.

WIDSITH

This epic is not intended to be the song of a single scop or minstrel; rather, it recounts the story of all minstrels who wander and glorify heroes and their actions. A long list of heroes is recited in the poem, including Alexander, Caesar, Attila the Hun, Hrothgar (who is a character in *Beowulf*), and Hagen (who appears in the *Nibelungenlied*).

Most scholars feel that *Widsith* is a composite of several lesser pieces and that the poem is not an autobiography. Obviously no minstrel could have visited rulers who were separated by several centuries. The first catalog of kings is of great antiquity, written at least as early as the sixth century. The remainder of the poem was written later and the "autobiographical" lines (see below) last of all. *Widsith,* in the form in which we have it, was put together in the late seventh or early eighth century. The manuscript—from the Exeter Book—is from the late tenth century.

The nature of the poem is clearly exemplified in these "autobiographical" lines:

> "I have journeyed over many strange lands in the wide world; I saw goodness and evil, I was separated from my children, I was away from my kindred, but I followed wisely. Thus it is that I can sing and tell a tale, and recount before everyone in the mead-hall how the noble of race treated me well." (lines 101–114)

These lines are perhaps the autobiographical intrusions of a later scop who added to the fragments of *Widsith*. They are not, however, related to other parts. This "word-horde" has more value as a catalog of the principal figures of the heroic age than as poetry.

THE FIGHT AT FINNSBURG (c. 750)

This poem, a fragment of about forty lines, was written at about the same time as *Beowulf.* The subject is a battle between the Frisians, led by King Finn, and the Danes, led by Hnaef. The Danes are treacherously attacked in a mead-hall, in which apparently they are guests, and they fight for five days. At this point the narrative is broken off but we learn from *Beowulf* that a truce is declared after Hnaef is killed. (See *The Finnsburg Episode* in Canto XVI of *Beowulf.*)

WALDERE (c. 750)

This poem survives in two fragments that presumably were parts of a longer poem concerning Walther of Aquitaine or

Walter of Spain. The first fragment is part of the maiden Hildegund's speech, in which she urges her lover, Walter, to fight the Frankish warrior, Hagen. The second fragment consists, chiefly, in Walther's reply. These fragments are important because of their relation to the great Volsung-Nibelungen sagas of Germany and Scandinavia.

EPICS AFTER BEOWULF

As late as the tenth century there are representatives of the epic tradition to be found. *The Battle of Brunanburh* is the entry in most of the manuscripts of the *Anglo-Saxon Chronicle* for the year 937. This narrative poem recounts the defeat of a combination of Norsemen and Scots by the Anglo-Saxons under King Athelstan, a successor of King Alfred. *The Battle of Maldon,* however, is a narrative poem that describes the defeat of the Anglo-Saxons by a contingent of Danes in the year 991. Maldon is fragmentary, although there is not too much missing. In both poems the battle scenes are gruesomely detailed, but they demonstrate the persistence of the institution of *comitatus* as something that the Anglo-Saxons still revered.

NON-HEROIC ANGLO-SAXON POETRY

GREAT OLD ENGLISH POEMS

Outside of the heroic traditions of *Beowulf,* there is a body of poetry which stands, in a few instances, amidst the great poetry of English literature. Some of the lyrics (called "elegies"), such as *The Wanderer* and *The Seafarer,* are worth the pains of learning Anglo-Saxon. It is difficult, perhaps impossible, to find a lyrical poem that rises above these with their finely wrought music and development. Their sophistication in the use of technical devices and their complexity of effects as works of art demonstrate the limitations of an idea of progress in art, for these can hardly be said to run behind later lyrics. The poets' entrance into the language of poetry in order to create there the life of their subjects is dazzling. In addition to the elegiac poetry, there is a significant body of religious poetry, in which is found the great poem *A Dream of the Rood.* It will help our perspective to survey these poems briefly.

ELEGIAC POEMS

As we noted earlier, the Germanic concept of destiny or fate (*wyrd*) was a very profound one to the extent that the deity Wyrd became confused with the Christian Almighty God. We shall examine sections in *Beowulf* that demonstrate this paradoxical intermingling of pagan and Christian, but the point is that the Anglo-Saxons regarded life as humanity's struggle against time (the great destroyer) and the passing glories of this earth. A poem devoted to the illusory and fleeting nature of life is called an elegy, and the poems thus written have been termed elegiac poems. Unlike the poems we usually call elegies, these poems are not concerned with personal death.

Many fine elegiac lines in *Beowulf* (for example, *The Survivor's Lament*) give evidence that the elegiac tradition is certainly no later than the seventh or eighth century. Contemplation of the vanished Romano-Briton civilization, or contemplation of the dying Anglo-Saxon society, may have inspired some of the melancholic, nostalgic outlook that is such a hallmark of elegiac verse.

THE WANDERER

We looked earlier at some of *The Seafarer* in the original and in Pound's version. Now let us consider the other great elegy, *The Wanderer,* which, on the face of it, "realistically" describes the spiritual journey of a wanderer (an *eardstapa,* meaning "earth-treader"). Now an exile out on the icy seas, he thinks back to the days when he served his lord (in the *comitatus* relationship), and he has a dream in which he bows to his lord and pledges his loyalty. His excited imagination is too great for sleep, however, and he is ripped from bliss and left in the empty, grim, lonely reality of his wandering on the icy sea. He calls to "old comrades" (who, as some critics suggest, are possibly seagulls) but they disappear in the air without a word. Now he laments the loss of his glorious past to the ravages of time in the *ubi sunt* ("Where are . . . ?") theme that is so important in medieval literature. (*Ubi sunt* were the beginning words of many medieval Latin poems, but the lines most familiar to us are those of the medieval French poet François Villon in his *Ballade:* "Where are the snows of yesteryear?" It was translated into English by Dante Gabriel Rossetti as "The Ballad of Dead Ladies.") Thus the wanderer asks: "Where now is the warrior? Where is the war-horse?" He concludes: ". . . those days have long ago rushed / Into the night of the past, as if they had never existed!" The wanderer comes to see that "all is wretchedness in the realm of the earth," and he has made his spiritual journey from *eardstapa* to a man of wisdom (*snotter on mode*). At the end he has moved into a transcendental Christian reality wherein comfort is possible.

INTERPRETATIONS OF THE WANDERER

There are diverse views on the particulars in the poem and at least three widely accepted and very different interpretations: (1) that the wanderer turns to Christian salvation; (2) that the poet, a Christian, uses the wanderer, a pagan, as an object for his dogmatism; and (3) that the poem is a Christian allegory, not the account of a real wanderer. But it is clear that the poem is in some sense a dramatic monologue—a complete dramatic experience conveyed to us through the words and thoughts of the person who endures it. Yet there is a separation of personae (of the speaking dramatic characters) in that we hear in the beginning, the middle, and the end, the voice of the poet-narrator. Also, the *eardstapa* has different voices, reflecting his spiritual development at different points in the poem. It seems likely that in half of Part I (encompassing half of the 115-line poem) he reflects on his happy past in his own voice but that the narrator seems to enter abruptly to tell of what happens in the subjective experience of the wanderer. We probably actually hear very little of the wanderer's voice.

THE WANDERER AND
OTHER OLD ENGLISH POETRY

This shifting about of voices is characteristic of much of Old English elegiac and narrative poetry and could suggest a special dramatic device, an accumulative method of composition (consistent with the oral tradition), or both. *The Wanderer* thus demonstrates to us some of the ways in which Old English poetry is structured. It poses a Christian world against a pagan world, personal experience against an allegorical use of experience. Unlike most of Anglo-Saxon poetry, *The Wanderer* is illusive in its presentation of subjective experience; the world of literal experience is seen through the mind and sensibility of the wanderer. Through the voices, diction, and special effects of the poem, we enter into his memory, dream, reason, imagination, and the final conceptualizing. In modern terms, we shift from a narrator's monologue to the wanderer's dramatic interior monologue and then to a third-person narrator's voice, which takes us through the sensibility—action—of the wanderer. (James L. Rosier's article [see Bibliography] gives a brilliant defense of this view and of the view that the poet employed "generative composition" [a method of composition in which the poetry is guided as much by words used, repeated and transformed, as by the experience in the poet's mind]. See The Elements of Anglo-Saxon Poetry for further discussion.)

OTHER POEMS: THEMES

The very personal sorrow or unhappiness that is found in, for example, *The Husband's Message* or *The Wife's Lament,* is not found in the above-mentioned elegies. In *The Wife's Lament,* a woman who has been separated from her husband by captivity voices her bitterness and loneliness:

> I could deluge the earth with my tears
> For grief and parting, for the unresting
> Heartache of melancholy . . .

The Husband's Message is less bitter but still pervaded by that personal melancholy of longing. The husband hopes to be reunited with his wife in the springtime, but for the present he "looks longingly":

> Come to a southbound vessel
> And away, on the waves to where
> Your husband, your lord, longs for you.

Another elegiac poem to which the scholars have given great attention is *Wulf and Eadwacer.* This is a brief, intense, passionate poem. Some critics have seen this poem as a sketch or fragment of a dramatic monologue. The few lines of *Wulf* treat of a woman who desires her lover, Wulf, and despises her husband, Eadwacer.

CHRISTIAN POEMS

In the writings of Bede we find the story of Caedmon, an illiterate cowherd who was employed by Hild, the abbess of Whitby. As the story goes, Caedmon retired from a banquet and went to sleep when an angel came to him and asked him to sing. In spite of his ignorance and dislike of singing, he sang a short phrase in praise of creating, quoted according to its "general sense" (and not the words) by Bede and now known as Caedmon's *Hymn:*

> Let us give praise to the Maker of heaven's kingdom, the power and end of our Creator, and the deeds of glory's Father. Let us sing how everlasting God, the Worker of all miracles, originally created the skies as a roof to cover the sons of man and how their almighty Protector gave them the earth for their home.

The poem is basically a series of epithets applied to God, but its delicate music gives it poetic value. One hears the music in Bessinger's fine recording. (See Bibliography.) According to Bede, Caedmon composed more lyrics on subjects found in Genesis and Exodus, on Christ's Incarnation, and on other religious and devotional subjects. If Bede is correct, then Caedmon is the first poet identified by name in English literature.

CAEDMONIAN POEMS

In the Junius manuscript there are epic poems surviving that agree with titles mentioned by Bede: two Genesis poems (A and B), Exodus, Daniel, and *Christ and Satan.* In the Exeter Book, the poem Azarias is associated with Daniel. These poems, since they were composed by several poets, belong to what is known as the Caedmon "cycle." Between them there are too many differences of style, dialect, and other elements for there to be a possibility that one poet composed them all. The poems of the Caedmon cycle are faithful to all of the scop's traditions—that is, in their use of alliteration, kennings, and so on. (See Elements of Anglo-Saxon Poetry in this guide.) The biblical figures assume the place that Beowulf assumes in the heroic epic. In the poem *Satan,* a certain sophistication of outlook is evidenced in the treatment of Satan; the sympathetic examination of his character—for all his evil—makes that poem a worthy forebear of Milton's *Paradise Lost*. The tendency to moralize imposes limitations and unevenness upon the poems of the Caedmon cycle, but still the poems stand out for their simplicity and vigor.

CYNEWULFIAN POEMS

The Cynewulfian poems, which follow the Caedmonian poems in time and literary progression, exhibit a greater Church influence than do their precursors. These are the first signed poems in English literature. Four of them—*Juliana, Elene, Christ,* and *The Fates of the Apostles*—have the signature Cyn(e)wulf written in isolated runic letters. All we know about this Cynewulf is that he was a cleric who lived around the year 800. In *Elene,* the poet's moral condemnation of himself is exaggerated; but after he had passed his youth, God gave him the gift of poetry and he has found his happiness. This is a suggestion of the Caedmon myth and indicates a familiarity on the part of the Cynewulfian poets (or at least Cynewulf) with the Caedmonian poems. The Cynewulfian poems have a greater degree of sophistication than even the most sophisticated of the Caedmonian poems (for example, *Satan*). The art of the poet has clearly broken away from some parts of bardic restriction, and there is a tendency to less obvious religiosity and moralizing than exists in the Caedmonian poems. It is significant to note that two of the poems have women as their central figures. Other poems that belong to the Cynewulf cycle are *Andreas,* two *Guthlac* poems, *A Dream of the Rood* (one of the great poems in our literature), *The Phoenix, The Harrowing of Hell,* and *The Bestiary* (*Phisiologus*). Scholars differ in opinion about whether many of the other poems to be found in Old English literature should be included in either the Caedmonian or Cynewulfian cycles.

POPULAR LITERATURE

The collection of *Riddles*—of which there are nearly a hundred in the Exeter Book—form much of the body of popular literature. There are also riddles, written in Latin, that are much

the same as their Anglo-Saxon relatives. In general, they picture common objects, phenomena, or persons, and the reader
or listener is left to identify the subject. The liking of primitive
peoples for riddles or conundrums is widespread, but many a
modern scholar has spent hours in puzzlement over some of
the riddles. Popular literature other than the *Riddles* is varied,
but a most significant other example is *The Riming Poem*.
This is almost the only extant poem in Anglo-Saxon literature
that uses end-rhyme as a poetic device. These rhymes are
antagonistic to the sense of the poem, and it has been
suggested that this poem is an experiment based upon Latin
hymns of the period that used rhyme.

OLD ENGLISH PROSE

Prose is a later development in civilization than poetry. Old English prose dates from the late ninth, tenth, and eleventh centuries, and its authors are usually known. It is useful to note here the landmarks in the history of prose.

King Alfred the Great (849–899): The "father" of Old English prose, he sought to make Wessex the focal point of culture. In attempting to make the vernacular English the national language, he translated and had translated important Latin texts, including Pope Gregory's *Pastoral Care,* Bede's *Ecclesiastical History,* St. Augustine's *Soliloquies,* Boethius' *Consolation of Philosophy,* and Orosiux's *Universal History.* These had a great effect on the development of later writers.

The *Anglo-Saxon Chronicle* (891): Discussed above, this document—also called *Old English Annals*—was set up by Alfred and is one of the primary sources for our historical study of England. It covers the period from 55 B.C. (Caesar's first invasion) to A.D. 1154 (the accession of Henry II).

Aelfric (c. 955–c. 1020): Abbott Aelfric, of Winchester and Oxfordshire, was the first truly accomplished prose writer in English. His purpose was to provide instruction in the principles of Christian life for those who did not read Latin. His important works are his 120 *Homilies* (a homily being a work that urges its readers to accept a specific moral view) and his translation of the first seven books of the Bible.

Wulfstan (died 1023): Bishop of London and then of Worcester, Archbishop of York, he also had significant diplomatic and literary careers. He is best remembered for his homilies, in which his prose style is accomplished and varied, employing at times such poetic techniques as rhyme and alliteration.

Latin Prose: Latin prose naturally flourished throughout the Old and Middle English periods. Most of it was didactic and of little literary value. The masterpiece of Anglo-Latin literature is Bede's *Historia Ecclesiastica Gentis Anglorum* (*The Ecclesiastical History of the English People*), discussed above. Other Anglo-Latin writers of note were: Alcuin (735–804)—author of commentary on Genesis; Aldhelm (c. 640–709)—writer of Latin verse and prose; Gildas (c. 516–c. 570)—historian; Nennius (late eighth century)—historian; Asser (died c. 909)—author of a biography of Alfred.

INTRODUCTION TO BEOWULF

UNITY

Although there is a considerable minority of dissenting opinions, it is generally agreed that *Beowulf* is a unified work—that is, a work whose elements are related to each other in such a way that the meaning of the work is derived from a consideration of the configuration or total configuration of these elements. To the modern reader, this unity may not seem perfectly obvious. In reading *Beowulf* we shall see a number of digressions made by the poet into genealogy and contemporary myth, obscure historical references, repetition of events, and unevenness of time. All of these things, by modern standards, are not always conducive to what Edgar Allan Poe called "unity of effect."

But the difficulties do not lie completely within the poem itself. Obviously the modern reader demands and expects something according to quite different tastes than the eighth-century Anglo-Saxon; and, historically speaking, the modern reader—even if extremely well-read—will encounter difficulties in placing *Beowulf* into a proper historical context. For the Anglo-Saxon audience, the historical digressions of *Beowulf* served to unify the epic with facts which were common knowledge (at least to the educated). Without a knowledge of the historical references, of course, much of the irony of *Beowulf* is lost. Secondly, the modern reader may not be quite so interested in the telling and retelling of Beowulf's exploits. Once would seem to be enough for a reader (or listener) interested in more subtle psychological motives for these actions. But the actions of Beowulf, his deeds and feats of glory, provide the chief source of interest to the Anglo-Saxon audience. *Beowulf* is addressed largely to the educated class of Anglo-Saxon society, but it must be remembered that this society was "newly settled," and not completely won away from its traditions of warlike spirit, aggressiveness, and the glories of battle. Indeed, the mood of melancholy, harking back to the "days of yore," prevails in much of *Beowulf*.

TRADITIONS

Another puzzling aspect of *Beowulf* to the logical-minded modern reader is the contradiction between elements of Germanic folklore interwoven with Christian morality and biblical history. As we shall see, Beowulf alternately places his faith in *wyrd* (fate or destiny) and the Lord God. When Beowulf remarks that "fate goes ever as it must," the implication is that humans have little free will but rather are creatures largely at the mercy of higher forces who generally use them as they will. Close to his death, Beowulf remarks that he has "endured his destiny." This is the Stoic resignation of a great warrior: within his limits, he has done what he can. But we also shall see that it is the "Lord God triumphant" who awards Beowulf the victory over Grendel's mother, the she-monster. The poet will inform us that the Danes should not expect relief from the scourges of Grendel because they have fallen away from the true God. Both Hrothgar and Hygelac give thanks to God for Beowulf's heroic victories over the monsters; and Beowulf himself—on the point of dying—gives thanks to God that he never has taken the life a kinsman.

It has been argued by critics that *Beowulf* was originally a pagan poem into which elements of Christian tradition and morality were interpolated. Modern scholarship has demonstrated, however, that the Christian elements are so pervasive in *Beowulf*—down to the imagery and language—that they represent no interpolation. Rather, the contradiction must be found in the society itself from which *Beowulf* emerged. The conversion of the Anglo-Saxons took place only a century and a half prior to the composition of *Beowulf*. Although its author was quite familiar with the Bible (which supposes that his audience was equally familiar), the Germanic traditions continued to persist. The poet, for example, has difficulty in deducing the genealogy of Grendel (a Germanic monster) from Cain, the "first murderer." And Wyrd, the Germanic deity of fate and destiny, is identified with the Lord God.

If, as it has been argued, a Christian society is the antithesis of a military society, then it would be difficult to imagine how the poet could interpolate any New Testament virtues into *Beowulf*. The Old Testament accounts of creation, the Flood, Adam and Eve, Cain and Abel, and so on would, of course, be accessible to the Anglo-Saxon apprehension. Not so easy, however, is a "turn-the-other-cheek" morality, or a parable of wheat and tares. Significantly, the poet—perhaps unconsciously—identifies some Christian virtues specifically with women. We shall see that Wealhtheow, the queen of Hrothgar, is a "peacemaker" (a role assigned to women, generally, in Anglo-Saxon court circles) and that in her speeches, she talks of honesty, friendship, and gentleness. The Christian sin of pride is treated at length in Hrothgar's discourse, and the vanities of the world are taken up in the brief episode, *The Survivor's Lament*. Other New Testament themes are touched upon, but never in a directly identifiable way (as in the sense that Lazarus would be mentioned, like Cain), which implies the gradual effusion of Christian morality into the categories of Anglo-Saxon thought. St. Augustine was ordered to proceed slowly with his conversion of Britain; and it is as if his task and the task of his successors was to be careful about pouring new wine into the old wineskins.

DIVISIONS

Beowulf must be regarded as one regards the epic of Achilles—that is, with respect to the larger context of historical time and place. The life of Beowulf in the epic has been seen by some critics as dividing it into two parts: the youthful Beowulf and the older Beowulf. The youthful Beowulf represents a hero without reputation, a young man eager to do great deeds and behave according to his sense of "form." He is ambitious, somewhat vainglorious, but generous and honest and not an oppressor of the weak. The older Beowulf is slightly weary of the struggles he has outlived, melancholy and contemplative but still possessed of the heroic spark to action, a good king to his people, a shepherd of his flock. While these two appearances of Beowulf may seem contradictory, the divisions are not absolute. One of the chief devices providing unity to *Beowulf* is the poet's almost tumultuous references to times present, past, and contemporary. The early cantos of *Beowulf* imply events that will happen in later cantos; later cantos refer back to earlier happenings; and, by way of digression, contemporaneous historical events are discussed and indicated. This is what one critic called "*Beowulf*'s forward, backward and sideways movement" in time.

Another interpretation divides the epic into three parts: Part I, Beowulf's struggle with Grendel; Part II, Beowulf's struggle with Grendel's mother; and Part III, Beowulf's struggle with the dragon. This focus on the three struggles of Beowulf easily lends itself to allegorical interpretations of *Beowulf*. In one sense, the struggles take the form of a "linear" development of the struggle between Good and Evil. We shall see that the monsters become progressively less susceptible to human apprehension (for example, compare Grendel's hand-to-hand struggle with Beowulf to the dragon's battle) and that they take on more unreal, abstractly identifiable qualities. In another sense, critics have taken the three struggles to represent parables of history. After the deaths of Grendel and his mother and also after the death of the dragon, the poet mentions portents of decay and doom for both the Spear-Danes and the Geats. The monsters may represent the objectification of internal revolutions or external political enemies (as some critics have contended) who finally will undo these nations.

BEOWULF'S ETHIC

In *Beowulf* runs the theme of *lof,* a nearly untranslatable word that means the praise and esteem of one's countrymen and contemporaries. A statement of this appears at the very beginning of *Beowulf:* "For among all peoples it is only through those actions which merit praise that a man may prosper." Fame, contends the poet, is the most permanent of all things in an impermanent world. Of all that one can have, fame survives everything of the transient and unstable. Modern philosophy might render *lof* as "objective immortality," in the sense that one's existence depends on someone's knowing it. Throughout the poem Beowulf is described as "hungry for fame," and the final eulogy praises Beowulf as "most desirous of reknown." Contrasted with this is the statement of Wiglaf that death is better than dishonor.

The idea of the illusory nature of the world is a favorite subject of Old English literature. To the Anglo-Saxon view of the warrior's struggles against the ebbing tides of life must be added the Christian other-worldliness to arrive at this particular admixture of "days of yore" and "veil of illusion." A good example of this melancholic sentiment occurs in *The Seafarer:*

> The wealth
> Of the world neither reaches to heaven nor remains.
> No man has ever faced the dawn
> Certain which of Fate's three threats
> Would fall; illness, or age, or an enemy's
> Sword, snatching the life from his soul.

Closely allied to the sentimental view of a transient and impermanent universe is the concept of *wyrd* (fate or destiny, as mentioned earlier). The God Wyrd stands behind the world of appearances, decreeing the vicissitudes of a person's life. Against *wyrd,* human power and knowledge cannot avail. The sermon of Hrothgar on pride—humanity's sin of reposing in the illusion of knowledge, or the illusion of its own powers—touches upon what the Greeks might have called *hybris,* a pride not unlike Christian pride but implying also that one has presumed upon the will of the gods. Pride, as it occurs in *Beowulf,* signifies the assignment of a faith to one's self that belongs rightfully to Wyrd. Hrothgar comments that for the prideful man "the world turns at his will; he does not know better." Hrothgar's sermon shows us also that no matter how much a person may have, in terms of wealth or power, he or she will depart the earth sadly and disillusioned. The point reminds us of a statement by Aeschylus: "Who sows the seeds of pride, reaps a harvest of tears."

The thoughtful reader may ask, then, what sustaining force is there behind the pessimistic consideration of humanity's impotence against a blind and impersonal fate? The question has been posed many times by the poet of *Beowulf*—and it is Beowulf himself who provides the answer. Beowulf believes that individuals must depend upon the tiny amount of free will at their disposal. They must make the right choices when they can, and then "unless a man is doomed beforehand, fate is likely to be favorable to the courageous . . ." Thus free will is equated with courage; and the courageous person, the person who can do deeds in the face of the world, will achieve fame (*lof*)—the only thing worth having. This concept may be difficult for the modern reader to accept because of the prevalence of such words as "individualism" and "freedom" in our vocabulary. As we have seen, however, the Anglo-Saxon conception of freedom was much more limited than is ours, and it involved itself with a person's courage, an ability to make the right or good choice in the face of the world.

BEOWULF
SUMMARY AND COMMENTARY

PROLOGUE

Beowulf opens with a genealogy of the royal house of the Spear-Danes, beginning with Scyld Sceafing, "Scyld, son of Sceaf." Scyld, who started his life as a foundling or castaway, later attained the heights of power and empire. The tendency to obscure the origins of Scyld is a mythical device, paralleled ironically in the myth of Oedipus. This obscurity renders a character more symbolic or general; it is found in modern fictional works, including Melville's *Billy Budd*.

Scyld, however, "was a good king," and it is fitting that his son Beowulf (not the Beowulf of this epic) should win fame throughout Scandinavia. "It is fitting," we are advised, "that a son should merit the honor of his father's comrades," a sentiment not uncommonly found in societies where the patriarchal family is the fundamental unit. The poem concludes its account of the eponymous Scyld with his death and funeral:

> At his destined hour, Scyld, the great striver,
> departed to go into the protection of the Lord.

Appropriately Scyld is borne away on the sea, just as he was borne on the sea to Denmark as a child. It is as if Scyld were regarded as a child of the ocean, the ocean symbolizing the future and primordial time. We are reminded of Tennyson's phrase, which he applies to Arthur (who is of equally obscure origins): "from deep to deep he goes."

An underlying motif in the introduction is the rise and fall of nations and the suggestion of earlier times that are wrapped in the veil of the mysterious. Significantly, the poet does not begin his account of Beowulf in medias res (as Homer began the *Iliad*) but rather refers in the first lines to "days of yore"— that is, to a time when heroes and demigods walked the earth.

Critics have taken reference of this sort (the Scyld episode) as a sort of paradoxical persistence of Anglo-Saxon tradition alongside an incipient Christian tradition. We shall see many more examples of this later in *Beowulf*.

CANTO I

After the death and funeral of Scyld Sceafing, his son Beowulf ruled the Spear-Danes for a long time, and subsequently the "lofty Healfdene," Beowulf's son, became ruler. From Healfdene sprang four children, three of whom are Heorogar, Hrothgar, and Halga. Hrothgar achieved glory and fame in war. It was his ambition to command a great mead-hall (a symbol or emblem of prowess in war and the obligation of a lord to his thanes), and he was successful: "In time it happened, early in his life, that it (the mead-hall) was constructed, of hall-houses the greatest." The name of the great mead-hall was Heorot, a name given it by Hrothgar himself. With the building of the great hall, Hrothgar pledged happiness and security to his subjects, and the kingdom settled down to peace and the enjoyment of listening to tales of the bards. The bards, called scops, sang of former times, back to the beginning of time when "the Almighty wrought the earth." The account of the creation in the book of Genesis is referred to in the singing of the "gleemen."

The peace and contentment of Hrothgar and his subjects was not to be permanent, however, because of a "fiend in Hell," who, angered by the singing of the bards, began to perpetrate crimes. Grendel, the "grim guest," is the monster who has descended from Cain, the first murderer, and who spreads evil and destruction wherever he goes.

COMMENT

Although there is no actual evidence for the existence of Scyld and his son Beowulf, the later Scyldings were apparently a dynasty ruling Denmark from around 550 to 650. Although the Sutton Hoo discovery has confirmed what may seem to be the fancies of the poet concerning the funeral of Scyld, there has been, as yet, no evidence that any of the Anglo-Saxon kings lived in such a hall as Heorot. The name "Heorot" signifies royalty and is derived from the word "Hart," meaning ringlike or regal. The incidents in Heorot indicate that the lord-thane relationship (the *comitatus* of Tacitus) is preserved and the relationship is clearly delineated. Hrothgar, the "ring-giver," distributes rewards and his faithful thanes expect such gifts in exchange for their services. It was the great shame of a lord (as noted earlier) should he ever be surpassed in valor by one of his thanes, and it was their great shame should they ever leave him on the battlefield.

The scop (minstrel or gleeman) entertains the feasting and mead-drinking warriors with songs accompanied by a harp. The poet hints of the destruction of Heorot, however, in the midst of his description of its beauty: "The hall towered high, curving like the horn: great heat from enemy fire awaited it." The hostile fire either will be spread by Grendel, a half-Germanic, half-Christian monster, or may be taken as a historical reference—that is, to a future time when Hrothgar's kingdom shall have been destroyed.

CANTO II

Enraged at the revelry at Heorot, Grendel invades the mead-hall and snatches up thirty of the sleeping warriors. He devours them whole and returns again the following evening. The fear inspired by Grendel's monstrous outrage is mentioned ironically by the poet: "Then another place was found by those who would sleep better." The war between the Danes and Grendel continues for twelve unremitting years. There is to be no peace between Grendel and the Danes, and he can be neither defeated nor bought off. The Danes invoked their ancient deities, and the poet mentions that the Danes were, at that time, not aware of the Christian God: ". . . they did not know the Creator, the Judge of actions, they did not know the Lord God . . ." And it is suggested that "woe befalls" the one who does not pray to the Christian God: "Do not let him to expect comfort nor anything to aid him. Good will go to him who, after his death, seeks the Lord . . ."

COMMENT

In this canto a contradiction is found between the monotheistic Christian beliefs presumed in earlier cantos and the deliberate statement that the Danes did not know the "Lord God." Historically this may refer to a time when the Danes backslid or fell away from the church, as when the Israelites, while Moses was being given the Ten Commandments upon Mount Sinai, fell away from their faith. On the other hand, and in line with other unsolved cruces, the passage may represent the persistence of Germanic tradition for those who either had not fully accepted the Christian dogma or had not accepted it at all. Nevertheless, it is likely that a Christian moral is indicated because, as the poet points out, no help shall be given to the one who fails to pray to the Lord God.

So great was the fear and misery of the Danes that it was openly voiced in song, we are informed. It is through these songs that news will reach Beowulf and he will decide to come to the rescue of Hrothgar.

CANTO III

When Beowulf, thane of Hygelac, hears of Hrothgar's misfortune, he decides to come to his aid. (Beowulf is not an Anglo-Saxon but a member of the Geats—a related Scandinavian people.) We shall see later that a special tie of friendship binds Hrothgar and Ecgtheow, the father of Beowulf. Beowulf's journey over the sea is brilliantly rendered by the poet:

Impelled over the waves by wind
The foamy prow like a bird
Sped onward till the next day's hour
Showed ocean shores shining, lofty hills,
Expansive shorelands.

Beowulf and his heroic followers are greeted by a Danish coast-guardsman who does not immediately recognize them. He asks them sternly but politely to identify themselves. In posing this question, the coast-guardsman gives an indication of his function: "For this I am placed at the extremity of land, that no enemies of the Danes may beach their ship-armies." Clearly, the guardsman is impressed with the noble appearance of Beowulf and his retainers. He remarks that he has never seen a "greater earl on earth." Still, it will be necessary for Beowulf to identify himself and explain his mission.

COMMENT

The Old English poets are at their best in describing the sea and journeyings over the sea and the passage here is no exception. The images of the sea in this section of *Beowulf* suggest images that appear in the elegiac poem, *The Seafarer* but lack the element of dread that could not, according to the heroic tradition, appear in the minds of Beowulf or his comrades.

Because of the abundance of petty kingdoms, warlike clans and tribes, and sea-riders of all descriptions, the Danes (and most coastal dwellers) stationed "coastal guards" to give alarm in case of invasion by a raiding party or army. Significantly, the character of the sea-raiders' strategy is rendered obvious by the term "sea-army." The raiders were both soldiers and sailors. We remember from Roman history that in the First Punic War the sea-army of the Romans defeated the superior seamanship of the Carthaginian navy, and so this type of strategy is not really new to military history.

The appearance of Beowulf is impressive to the coast-guardsman, and we may contrast the young Beowulf here with the older Beowulf who will appear later. As a young man, Beowulf is seen to be vigorous, somewhat vain, aggressive, noble, and good. Some of these qualities will ripen through maturity; others will become obscured entirely by his subsequent melancholy. Note that the Anglo-Saxon conception of *lof* or desire for worldly fame makes these characteristics typical of heroes.

CANTO IV

Beowulf identifies himself as a follower of Hygelac and as a member of the Geats. His father is Ecgtheow, who is well known to every sage and minstrel. Through kind feeling of Hrothgar, Beowulf says, he seeks to defend him and show him how the foe may be overcome. The guardsman directs them on to Hrothgar and promises that their ship will be defended. From Beowulf's noble words and bearing the guardsman perceives that he is no enemy of the Danes.

COMMENT

Beowulf makes reference to his famous father and also to a bond that exists between himself (through his father) and Hrothgar, referred to as Healfdene's son. The implication is that Ecgtheow and Hrothgar knew each other earlier.

The function of the coast-guardsman is, in addition to watching for sea-raiders or "sea-armies," to defend friendly ships against despoilment. As Beowulf is a noble hero, and his companions are mighty warriors, so also is the character of his ship once again denoted: ". . . your ship, newly tarred . . ." It will be remembered from Canto III that a "wave traverser good" was prepared for Beowulf's journey and that the noble ship is not without the significance, in terms of the epic, that would be attached to Jason's Argo (or, similarly, Arthur's sword

Excalibur). The point is that the implements or posses-
sions of a hero become imbued with an almost miraculous or holy significance.

CANTO V

After walking up a stone-paved road, Beowulf and his band
arrive at Heorot. The bearing and dress of the group are impressive and Hrothgar's servant and messenger exclaims:
"I have never seen strangers or men any prouder." Beowulf
identifies himself again and requests an audience with Hrothgar.
A noble Wendel, Wulfgar, tells him that he will advise Hrothgar
who they are and why they have come and that he will return
with Hrothgar's answer. Wulfgar is valorous and wise and "he
knew the usage of a court." He probably is court chamberlain
as well as Hrothgar's advisor. He suggests to Hrothgar that the
visitors be granted an audience because they appear to be
worthy—especially their chief, Beowulf.

COMMENT

That the Danish court is more than a collection of ill-
mannered warriors is obvious here. There is a definite
court "usage" or etiquette, and a sense of "form" is manifest. The proud bearing of Beowulf and his band at first
seems to presume upon the honor of the court; it
requires the services of the court-wise Wulfgar as inter-
mediary to see that the dignity of neither Hrothgar's court
nor his visitors is offended.

CANTO VI

Hrothgar remembers Beowulf as a child and mentions
Beowulf's father, Ecgtheow, with some detailed knowledge.
He is given hope by the arrival of Beowulf because he knows
him to be of noble parentage. Hrothgar offers treasure to
Beowulf and his warriors if they are able to rid his land of the
monster. Beowulf hails Hrothgar and in grandiose terms
delineates his errand to rid the land of the Grendel monster
and to make Heorot useful once again. Beowulf recites that

he avenged the Weders' quarrels and asks for the honor of challenging the monster and purifying Heorot. For his part, Beowulf says, he will trust in the "Lord's doom" and will bear neither shield nor spear. If the monster triumphs, he continues, then it shall only be through his death, and he will have no need to hide is head. Beowulf closes his petition with the mention of *wyrd,* implacable fate: "Fate goes ever as it must."

COMMENT

Hrothgar's detailed knowledge of Beowulf's father has been suggested earlier by Beowulf's own statements. On the basis of this knowledge, Hrothgar has asked that Wulfgar welcome Beowulf and his followers. Thus the suggestion of the introductory canto—that is, that a father's son "should merit the honor of his father's comrades"—is shown to be true of Beowulf. In the Germanic tradition Beowulf does not understate what his deeds have been or what he intends to do. Speaking to Hrothgar, Beowulf says that since Grendel does not use weapons, he also disdains them. Continuing, Beowulf mentions his "qualifications" for battling Grendel: He has wrestled victoriously with sea-monsters. Here we see Beowulf as almost pure hero in the tradition of Achilles: proud, disdainful, and ambitious.

CANTO VII

Hrothgar continues his reminiscences about Beowulf's father and recounts Ecgtheow's great feat of killing Heatholaf, interweaving an account of his own quarrels with the Wylfings. Abruptly, Hrothgar's conversation changes to the subject of his own present sorrows and tribulations, for which the monster Grendel is directly the cause. In his old age, Hrothgar says, he has seen his mead-hall deprived of retainers and warriors; Heorot is now useless. Hrothgar then invites Beowulf to speak what is on his mind and to partake in the feasting and mead-drinking. Beowulf, his band, and the Danes sit down to drink and to listen to the songs of the scops.

COMMENT

Hrothgar's discursive rambling may be interpreted as a clever device of the poet to demonstrate Hrothgar's senility (he is referred to in Canto V as "old and hoary"). More probably, however, the side references pertain to epics or tales well known to the listeners or readers of *Beowulf* and serve to unify the poem with other elements in Germanic folklore. This method of side references or digressions to contemporaneous tales is a deliberate literary device in works of the Middle Ages. Such works as Eschenbach's *Parzifal* abound with them. (The interrelation of characters in the works of a single author is a more recent development of this device and is seen in the works of such authors as Leo Tolstoy and James Joyce.)

Hrothgar invites Beowulf to sit down with his own warriors "and unbind with mead thy valiant breast. . . . " It is an invitation to recount his own deeds of valor publicly in the form of a traditional Germanic *beot* or boast. It will be a public proclamation of the deeds Beowulf will undertake and as such may be thought of as providing a "contract" between Beowulf and Hrothgar.

CANTOS VIII AND IX

During the feast, Beowulf is taunted by Unferth, who is jealous of his glory. Unferth asks Beowulf if he is the same one who was bested by Breca, chief of the Brondings, in a swimming contest. Contending that Breca had more strength than Beowulf, Unferth dares Beowulf to spend a night in Heorot. Beowulf replies with a different account of the contest with Breca. Theirs was a youthful venture, Beowulf contends: "When we were younger we agreed and promised (we were both youths) that we should venture our lives upon the ocean . . . . " Beowulf recounts that they had only swords to defend themselves against the sea-monsters and that they swam together for five nights in icy waters before they became parted.

Beowulf was attacked by a monster, who dragged him to the bottom of the sea and was killed by Beowulf's own hand. Subsequently, Beowulf describes how he killed nine monsters. Then, overcome with fatigue, he was borne by the sea to the land of the Finns. Breca, Beowulf contends, never achieved a feat equal to this. Beowulf taunts Unferth with the murder of his brothers and says that for these crimes Unferth shall suffer in Hell. Furthermore, Beowulf contends, Grendel has no fear of the Spear-Danes. He then boasts that a Geat shall overcome the monster. The traditional Germanic *beot* (warrior's boast) is given by Beowulf: "I shall perform deeds of noble valor or meet my end in this very hall." Wealhtheow, Hrothgar's queen, now appears. She gives the cup to her husband, then to his retainers, and then to Beowulf, thanking God that he has arrived to save them. She has trust in him, she says. "She thanked God . . . that the power to trust in any warrior had overtaken her, for succor against crimes." Beowulf takes the cup and restates the pledge he took when he started upon his journey.

His words please Wealhtheow, and the retainers and people rejoice. Abruptly, Hrothgar rises to make a speech before retiring. He affirms his trust in Beowulf, asks him to be mindful of glory and show his valor. Never before has he turned command of Heorot over to anyone else, he says. Hrothgar promises Beowulf "no dearth of desirable things, if you escape with your life from this deed of valor."

COMMENT

The character of Unferth is somewhat contradictory. He is described as jealous and sarcastic, and to him is imputed perhaps the most heinous of all crimes, fratricide. Later, as we shall note, Beowulf accepts the sword called Hrunting generously offered him by Unferth for use against Grendel's mother. Unferth is a *thyle*—that is, roughly, an orator or spokesman of Hrothgar, although it seems that his role is more that of inciting the warriors to a great pitch of boasting. His personality is not unlike that of the spidery Thersites in the *Iliad*, a character whose function is to make thrusts against Ulysses and the other heroes.

As we have seen, Unferth does incite Beowulf to recount the Breca episode (Breca, incidentally, is mentioned in the poem *Widsith*), and we are given further evidences of Beowulf's valor and prowess. It is significant in terms of Beowulf's reputation that the Breca episode is veiled in obscurity, for we shall see that Beowulf—to his contemporaries—does not yet possess a great reputation; in fact in his homeland just the contrary is true. The Danes, however, are well pleased with Beowulf when the festivities end. The respect accorded Beowulf is clearly evidenced in the statement made by Wealhtheow. Her statements also may indicate a certain tendency to idealize the woman; possibly, therefore, her character harks forward to later in the Middle Ages and the concept of "romantic love."

CANTO X

Hrothgar and his warriors then depart from the hall, leaving Beowulf and his comrades to await the monster. Beowulf removes his armor and sword, handing his equipment to an attendant and repeating the boast that he will meet the monster unarmed: "I do not regard myself less powerful in strength or warlike deeds than Grendel does himself." Beowulf's companions are not so assured of the outcome of the battle as their confident leader, however. As the poet relates: "Not one of them thought he would ever be seeking his homeland again." Beowulf lies down to an (apparently) untroubled sleep, a distinct contrast to his fearful comrades. "From afar in the murky night," Grendel, referred to as the "shadow walker," approaches.

COMMENT

It is interesting to note the contrast between the boastful, confident Beowulf and his hitherto proud companions, who have become more like ordinary people. In this, as in previous sections, the nearer in time we are carried to the appearance of Grendel, that foul monster from the reaches of Hell itself, the more purely heroic does the character of Beowulf become and the greater the contrast between him and those around him. In Beowulf's reply to the Danes, he contrasts the impotent Danes with a "man of the Geats," and now we see the transcendence of Beowulf—in heroic proportions—even to those of his own tribe.

Beowulf's companions are thinking about home, possibly lamenting the fact that they ever undertook the journey. Beowulf, on the contrary, thinks only of the glory as he settles down to sleep. This contrast creates a great deal of tension—especially considering the beliefs of the Anglo-Saxon mind at this period—because of the fearful followers, the unconcerned hero, and the monster lurking from afar. It is Beowulf's faith in *wyrd* (fate or destiny) that seemingly has transformed itself into a faith in God: "It has been truly demonstrated that Almighty God rules the race of men." This statement, however, made by the poet as an observation (typical of the poet's entrances into the poetry), is well in keeping with statements made by Beowulf later and demonstrates Beowulf's (as well as the Anglo-Saxon) alternate faith in Wyrd and God. It is Beowulf's faith in Wyrd/God that lends to him credence as a character and that will resolve his apparent lack of concern with the power of Grendel or loss of his own life. This, of course, is not to be confused with Beowulf's courage, the positive manifestation of his faith.

CANTO XI

Grendel comes stalking from the moor, smashes down the door of Heorot with "fire-hard hands," and stands amidst the sleeping warriors with a horrid flame standing from his eyes. From the "kindred band of sleeping warriors" Grendel snatches one man and devours him. Grendel reaches toward Beowulf and finds himself enmeshed in the warrior's stronger grip. Now fearful, Grendel longs to flee, but Beowulf does not remit his grasp. As the monster attempts to escape, the hall barely can stand the reverberations of the terrible struggle. Outside, the Danes are terrified by the awesomeness of Grendel's wailings.

COMMENT

In this canto Grendel appears as an incarnation of Satan himself. He is described as "a wicked spoiler of men," "the fiend," and one with "fire-hard hands," "from whose eye a horrid flame stood." Further, he is referred to as a "miserable wight," "a fell wretch," and "the criminal." Thus, we should not be more hesitant in regarding Grendel as Satan himself—based on these terms—than the original listeners. The origins of Grendel are equally as allusive of the Christian Satan and Christian Hell. Grendel comes "stalking from the moor," a mysterious region where, it was mentioned earlier, the unbaptized dare not enter. Grendel is a creature of night, a "shadow walker," and his place of habitation is in the mid-earth of the world's regions. The "fire-hard hands" and the "horrid light" may refer indirectly to the fires of Hell. Significantly, Grendel wishes to escape Beowulf's grip and retreat to his subterranean cavern, but he cannot.

Beowulf himself, however, does not escape from the abundance of fearful imagery cast over the monster. The angry Beowulf is one of "the warlike beasts." He is one of the "fierce ones," and it is suggested that the wrath of Beowulf is no less terrible to behold than the lust of the "pernicious spoiler." Finally, Canto XI closes with the monster's wail of defeat, which terrorizes the Danes. This forms an effective contrast to the voice of God heard at the beginning of time and of the Word that was heard even to the bottom of the abyss. The mournful shriek of Grendel may be taken as the shrieking of Satan himself, symbolizing his defeat and the fact that he is bound to Hell forever.

CANTO XII

The companions of Beowulf, awakened by the struggle, rally to defend their lord, but their swords are useless against the monster because he has cast a spell on them. Finally, Grendel tears his arm out of its socket in his struggle to be free, and the creature runs into the night, screaming in pain and terror. Grendel returns to the fens, knowing that he is dying. When Beowulf sees that Grendel is vanquished and is fleeing, he celebrates and rejoices in his own valor. Beowulf fastens Grendel's arm (which had been left behind) high upon the wall of the mead-hall.

COMMENT

The struggle between Beowulf and Grendel is an intensely personal struggle in which neither of the combatants uses weapons. It is almost as if it were a struggle between the wills of the adversaries themselves. Significantly, Beowulf's comrades are able to offer him no aid, and their swords are useless against the monster. Beowulf is satisfied to know that he has triumphed; he leaves it up to his comrades to follow the trail of the monster's blood.

CANTO XIII

The warriors of the Danes gather from far and near on the next morning to view the trophy and praise the valor of Beowulf. Hrothgar is also praised as a good king. The exploits of Beowulf are sung. Then a tale from the

Nibelungenlied is introduced; it concerns Sigemund, who destroyed a great dragon and thereby gained a great treasure. There follows a tale about King Heremod, presumably of the dynasty preceding the Scyldings. When this is concluded, all return to Heorot to view the trophy. There Hrothgar is joined by Wealhtheow and her maidens.

COMMENT

In the true Germanic tradition, the great victory is followed by feasting and celebrating, and songs are sung about the great deeds of heroes. The story of Sigemund may seem to be out of place here; but it must be remembered that such digressions served to make *Beowulf* more real to its listeners or readers, who would naturally be more familiar with such references than the modern student. The episode also has parallels with Beowulf's own adventure.

CANTO XIV

Hrothgar goes into Heorot and looks at the arm of the monster. He speaks about the misery and grief brought to his kingdom by Grendel and of the great feat of valor performed by Beowulf. Hrothgar tells Beowulf that hereafter he will love him as a son and that Beowulf will not lack "of desirable worldly things / that I have power over." Beowulf then describes his conflict with the monster and states that the creature will surely find great doom from the Almighty Creator. Unferth (Ecglaf's son) is silent as all affirm that no sword or weapon could equal the feat performed by Beowulf with his bare hands.

COMMENT

in Hrothgar's speech, thanks is given to the Almighty, recalling the words of the poet before the appearance of the monster: "It is truly shown that Almighty God rules the race of men." Hrothgar, as evidence of his great feeling for Beowulf, offers a reward greater than even all the gold and treasures that also will be awarded: He takes Beowulf into the bonds of kinship as a son.

Beowulf is more modest in this section than when he had undertaken his *beot* (boast) of his great accomplishments and promises. His account of the battle with Grendel is given simply and parallels the account given earlier in the poem. Significantly, we do not hear from Unferth as he views the monster's arm and nails of "steel."

CANTO XV

It is ordered that Heorot be cleansed, repaired and decorated for the feast that will follow. Golden tapestries are hung on the walls; food and drink in plenty are provided. Hrothgar presents Beowulf with a banner, a breastplate, and a helmet. After Beowulf drinks to the health of Hrothgar, he is presented with eight stallions and eight jeweled saddles to be added to his gifts. One of the saddles, inlaid and adorned with jewels, is Hrothgar's own, which he rode to war.

COMMENT

The giving of gifts from lord to thane was the accepted (and commonly expected) practice, and it formed part of the institution of comitatus. Beowulf, of course, has undertaken to defeat Grendel partly because of Hrothgar's bond with Ecgtheow and partly because Beowulf seeks fame. As an exception to court procedure and "usage," Beowulf is permitted to partake of the cup before Hrothgar's own retainers. This is another honor added to Beowulf.

We remember from Canto IV that Beowulf promised to "purify" Heorot and rid it of the monster. Similarly and materially, Heorot is purified after Grendel's vanquishment by the removal of blood-stains and all evidences of the monster. Only the arm is permitted to remain as both trophy and reminder. Thus Heorot is purified in a symbolic way from Sin, as some critics have claimed, and the purification is also carried out physically by the cleaning of the great hall.

CANTO XVI

The giving of gifts is continued in this canto and Hrothgar offers to pay in gold for the man who was killed. Following is a brief reference to Wyrd, and it is obvious here (once again) that the Anglo-Saxons identified Wyrd and the Christian God into one director of humanity: "The creator ruled the race of men as he still does." Singing begins, and the minor narrative "The Lay of Finn" (also known as the *Finn Episode*) is heard. "Hrothgar's hero," the Scyldling Hnaef, is killed, and the Frisian King, Finn, loses subsequent battle to Hengest. On the funeral pyre of Hnaef, Hildeburh, the Danish wife of Finn, places her own sons with great cries of sadness.

COMMENT

The episode concerning Finn, Hengest, and Hnaef is the traditional account (see Early History of England) of incidents relating to King Hnaef of the Danes and his visit to Finn, King of Frisia. A band of Finn's followers treacherously attacked the Danes as they slept in their mead-hall; a fierce fight ensued, lasting five days. This is taken from the epic *The Fight at Finnsburg* (see chapter on Heroic Literature above), which informs us that during the five days "none of the comrades fell and they held the door." We can see that the fight was essentially a standoff. From *Beowulf* we learn that eventually Hnaef was killed and that Hengest (Hnaef's successor) concluded a truce.

It has been suggested that the *Finn Episode* (and *The Fight at Finnsburg*) refer to a historically existent invasion of the Frisians by the Anglo-Saxons in the first half of the fifth century. As we have seen, this tradition is incorporated in Bede's writings, and Bede himself took the tradition from Gildas. Further corroborative evidence (or at least a cross-reference) is found in a text of the *Chronicle.*

In *Beowulf* it is suggested that the truce between the Frisians and the Danes is an uneasy one at best: "If any of the Frisians should call this feud to mind by speaking boldly, then the sword-edge shall appease it." We can readily see the two tribes living side by side amidst suspicion and desire for revenge. Finn, according to tradition, is eventually (as we shall see in the next canto) killed by the Danes.

CANTO XVII

The *Finn Episode* continues. Hengest remains all winter with the Frisians while the Danish warriors return home. When the Danish warriors return in the spring with reinforcements, Hengest breaks the truce and kills Finn, seizing Hildeburh and Finn's treasure. The scop concludes his song; then Wealhtheow appears. A passing reference to Unferth, the *thyle* (speaker, orator) is made: "He possessed great courage but had not been honorable to his kinsmen in sword-play." Wealhtheow gives the cup to Beowulf, who sits between her sons Hrethric and Hrothmund.

COMMENT

With the conclusion of the Finn Episode, Wealhtheow makes another appearance and again gives the cup to Beowulf. She enjoins good fortune upon him and advises him to dispense gifts while he may and leave his fortune and his kingdom to his children. Her advice is somewhat ironic, inasmuch as Beowulf will have no blood descendants, but neither Wealhtheow nor Beowulf is aware of the irony.

The parenthetical appearance of Unferth in a place of honor at the foot of his lord is, apparently, in preparation for his later appearance. As we have seen, he is no longer "jealous of glory," but rather "possessed of great courage," or mettlesome spirit, although it is again admitted that he did not use his kinsmen fairly. The contradictory qualities of Unferth sometimes lead the reader to suppose that this enigmatic character is the victim of unfounded rumors because, other than the charges laid against him, he is courageous and generous. Significantly, however, Unferth never denies the charges laid against him, leading the reader to suppose that he possibly has no defense. It is obvious that he is held in a certain awe and fearful respect, which could be directly due to the terribleness of his crimes.

CANTO XVIII

Wealhtheow gives Beowulf gifts of a corselet, rings, and a magnificent collar that the poet describes as "the largest of those on earth I have heard tell." The gifts received by Beowulf are compared to the treasure hoard of Hama. The collar received by Beowulf eventually will be worn by Beowulf's uncle, Hygelac the Geat, when he falls in a war against the Frisians. Wealhtheow asks Beowulf to be a guide to her sons and again enjoins fortune upon him, as well as long life and happiness. At the end of Wealhtheow's speech, an ominous foreboding of further calamity appears: ". . . the men drank wine, ignorant of fate or how grim calamity had befallen many men." Hrothgar departs to his court after evening, and the warriors sleep in Heorot with their armor as they did in former days according to their custom.

COMMENT

The speech of Wealhtheow is in direct contrast to the indication of doom appearing in the second half of this canto. Wealhtheow, the "Scylding's dame," is, perhaps, the personification of Woman to an extremely masculine, warlike society. She ever appears as humble, trusting, domestic, and subordinate to her lord Hrothgar.

Wealhtheow perhaps never becomes so abstract as to be a symbol for Goodness and Virtue; but in her speeches she refers to gentleness, goodness, faithfulness, and friendship. St. Augustine believed that women could be great spiritual agents for the Good, and Wealhtheow is a clear embodiment of this idea in *Beowulf.*

The warriors, unaware that something is about to happen, prepare Heorot by clearing benches and spreading the skins of animals on the floor. As is their custom, they retire with their weapons near them. The warriors, ironically, believe that things have returned to "normal" and everything is the way it "used to be," and so they go to sleep as usual.

CANTO XIX

Grendel's mother, the avenger of her son's death, appears. Her descent is traced from Cain, again referred to as the "first murderer." The warriors are amazed at her appearance: "There was an immediate relapse to the warriors when Grendel's mother rushed in. . . . " Seizing one of the warriors, she retreats to the fen. Significantly, the kidnapped warrior was one of Hrothgar's dearest comrades, a "powerful shield-warrior." Grendel's mother also takes her son's arm down from the wall before she flees. When that is noticed, a great cry arises from Heorot.

Beowulf, who has been given his own quarters, is not sleeping at Heorot. He is summoned to the presence of Hrothgar and, unaware of what has been happening, asks Hrothgar in all innocence if he had an easy night.

COMMENT

The genealogy of Grendel's mother as a descendant of Cain compels a response. Beowulf must do battle in recapitulation (as we might expect) of the genealogy of Grendel himself. From the fratricide, Cain, "the first murderer," spring demons, *eotins* (giants, monsters), and sprites. The underlying motif of evil and accompanying images of darkness and creatures of the underworld appear again.

The aspect of Heorot is changed completely after the appearance of Grendel's mother. Whereas there had been much feasting and merrymaking, now "sorrow had become renewed in the dwellings." This has been prepared for by the statements toward the last part of the previous canto (statements that contrast with the optimistic sentiments of Wealhtheow) and demonstrates the impotence and tragic situation of humanity in the world. That this theme need not necessarily be a pessimistic view of the Anglo-Saxons is discussed elsewhere (cf. Introduction to *Beowulf*). Suffice it to say that Beowulf, a believer in *wyrd* and in the will of God, does not take a pessimistic outlook, indeed, paradoxically opposing faith in himself as hero against the implacable forces around him.

CANTO XX

Hrothgar brushes aside Beowulf's inquiry after his happiness, saying that the sorrow of the Danes is renewed. The comrade of Hrothgar, Aeschere, is dead at the hands of Grendel's avenger. Hrothgar recounts an old legend of two monsters that inhabit the moor and walk by night. They are reported to live in a bottomless pool that is not far from Heorot. Hrothgar believes the two monsters of the legend to be Grendel and his mother. Beowulf is asked by Hrothgar to seek out Grendel's mother where she lives and to destroy her. If he performs this second great feat, then Hrothgar promises to reward Beowulf even as he did after the defeat of the first monster.

COMMENT

The female monster, though less powerful that her son, is shielded in her watery retreat. It is obvious that Beowulf will be at considerable disadvantage should he go there to seek her out. It is not known exactly where Grendel's mother lives, except somewhere in the fathomless pool: "There is living no one so wise of the children of men who knows the bottom."

The symbolic interpretation suggested by several critics is that Grendel's mother (and by implication, Grendel himself) is identified with Evil, just as Beowulf is identified with Good. Beowulf will fight in the forbidden realms of the powers of darkness, and it is suggested that he might not return: "I will reward you with money for your strife and with treasures as I did before and with twisted gold, if you come away." If, as other critics claim, the *Beowulf* epic represents the Christian theme of fall and redemption, then Beowulf's descent into the underworld lair of Grendel's mother surely represents his descent into Hell or, even more symbolically, represents in Germanic form Christ's descent into Hell. On another level it has been suggested that Beowulf's descent into Grendel's lair is taken from Virgil's account of Aeneas's descent into the netherworld. (Evidence for these interpretations depends on a wider textual examination than may be given here, but the interested student is advised to refer to the Bibliography for more references on the subject.) In any case, the heroic tradition determines that Beowulf shall undertake what others could not and that—because he is unique—he has hope of escaping. It is this implication that sustains Beowulf in his role as hero.

CANTO XXI

Beowulf replies kindly to Hrothgar's request, saying that it is better for all that a friend be avenged rather than mourned. Beowulf philosophically remarks that all people must meet their end and that all must do their works before that time if they hope for anything in the future. Beowulf promises to

seek out the monster and pledges that she shall not escape
into the earth's bosom, into the mountain's forests, or under
the floor of the ocean. Hrothgar thanks Beowulf and accom-
panies him and a group of warriors across the moor to the
fathomless pool. There they find the bloody head of Aeschere
and see firedrakes and sea-dragons swimming in the pool.
One of the dragons is killed and brought ashore. Beowulf
dons his variegated armor, "wondrously made . . . in days of
yore." Unferth generously lends Beowulf his sword, Hrunting,
which "never in battle was untrue to any man." Unferth
remarks that he had never lent the sword to a better warrior,
although it would not be the first time that the sword had
achieved a work of valor. Unferth also excuses himself for
words spoken when he was under the influence of strong
drink. Since, however, he will not go beneath the waves, his
reputation—unlike that of Beowulf—is forfeit.

COMMENT

The gentle, generous replies of Beowulf before his meet-
ing with Grendel's mother sharply contradict his boastful statements and promises before he met her son. The
character of Unferth has changed, too, from a spiteful
provoker to an apologetic and generous comrade. It is
almost as if all the characters have been softened by
Wealhtheow's admonishment to be gentle. Still, Beowulf
does not "care for death," and his belief in *wyrd* continues to prevail.

Beowulf dons his chain-mail, byrnie (a coat of mail),
and hauberk, which had been fashioned by a great smith
in "days of yore." At once this reference harks back to
the Grecian deity Hephaestus, who fashioned the armor
of Achilles, and forward to the great armor-smith
Trebuchtet, who fashioned the armor of so many great
knights of the Arthurian cycle.

CANTO XXII

Beowulf announces his readiness and asks Hrothgar to be a guardian of his comrades should he lose his life. He asks also that the treasure he has received be sent back to his lord Hygelac in the event of his death. Beowulf promises Unferth that he will "obtain fame with Hrunting or be taken by death." Thereupon Beowulf jumps into the pool and descends for nearly a day before he reaches the bottom. Grendel's mother advances toward him and then seizes him. Beowulf is protected by his ring-mail, but he is clutched so tightly by the monster that he cannot use his weapons. Grendel's mother flees with Beowulf toward her dwelling, and Beowulf sees around him many strange and antagonistic monsters. Finally he finds himself in a "hostile hall," the dwelling-place of the monster. Attacking the monster with his sword, Beowulf rings it on her head, but its blade is turned aside: Hrunting will do no damage, failing for the first time. Beowulf casts aside the sword and trusts to his hand-grip of power. The she-monster, however, thrusts Beowulf to the ground and tries to stab him with her dagger. Again Beowulf is protected by his sturdy ring-mail, without which he should surely have perished.

COMMENT

The struggle between Beowulf and Grendel's mother assumes a more supernatural aspect here than did the earlier battle. Beowulf plunges into the pool and descends for nearly a day—a superhuman feat in itself— and is protected from harm by his "wondrously wrought" armor. The armor becomes almost a symbol of a spell of protection enveloping Beowulf, keeping him from harm. Beowulf is exhausted, "weary of mood," by his descent into the pool and by his struggles. The she-monster, on her home battleground, is the stronger of the two combatants; furthermore, she seems to be aided by all the fell powers of Hell. But just as Beowulf is protected physically from the powers of darkness, so does the decision of "holy God in war triumphant" award to Beowulf victory over Grendel's mother and life. As we shall see, however, it is no mere gift that is given to Beowulf through the decision of God but something held out, still to be won through the efforts of the hero.

CANTO XXIII

On the point of death, Beowulf spies a miraculous sword among the collection of weapons. It is a sword fashioned by giants, greater than any weapon ever used by humans. Seizing the sword, Beowulf severs the monster's head. Beowulf then finds the body of Grendel and cuts its head from its body. Meanwhile, Hrothgar and his warriors, who have remained above, see the pool churning and growing bright with blood. Concluding that Beowulf has died, they return sadly to Heorot. Beowulf's companions remain, gazing sadly upon the crimson surface of the water. Suddenly Beowulf, with the monster's head in one hand, rises to the surface; there he is joyously received by his comrades. All return to Heorot, where Beowulf presents the monster's head to the king and queen.

COMMENT

It is interesting that Beowulf severs the head of the dead Grendel, because this incident probably refers to an old pagan belief that the only sure means of killing an ogre was to sever its head from its body with a magic sword. The "magic" sword is one more "miraculous" element in the account of Beowulf's battle with Grendel's mother. It stands in contrast to the personal struggle between Beowulf and Grendel, where Beowulf disdained the use of all armor and weapons. In a manner of speaking, the struggle had assumed more abstract proportions, furnishing evidence for those critics who see in *Beowulf* an allegory of the struggle between Good and Evil. If this interpretation is correct, then, Beowulf becomes identifiable with Christian Goodness, and Grendel's mother becomes the personification of Evil.

From the Christian standpoint, Hrothgar and his warriors lack faith and, convinced that Beowulf has died, return to Heorot, lamenting. Beowulf's comrades cannot leave, however, so strong is their attachment to their lord, but there is little they can do. Perhaps, according to the tradition of *comitatus,* they realize that they must descend into the depths to avenge Beowulf if he has died, but clearly the task is too great for mortal warriors.

CANTO XXIV

Beowulf offers the head of the monster to Hrothgar and describes the battle that has taken place. He gives Hrothgar the hilt of the miraculous sword taken from Grendel's lair and promises that all are now safe from invasion by the monsters. Hrothgar studies the runic inscriptions on the sword-hilt, which is described as the work of giants who existed before the Flood. He then delivers a long sermon on pride, eulogizing Beowulf as a benefit to his people and to the Danes and contrasting him to the evil king Heremod, who killed his own retainers and perverted the lord-thane institution. Heremod felt no joy and he received no respect from men, regardless of how he advanced in his power. Heremod, a person who trod upon wrongful paths, provides an example from whom all can profit.

COMMENT

Inasmuch as the story on the hilt of the miraculous sword is written in runes, it may be taken to pertain to elements of Germanic mythology, although the mythical battle of the giants is a common story in the folklore of many peoples. Interwoven with this is a reference to the Flood of the book of Genesis and to the Old Testament's Lord God.

The theme of fame is touched upon by Hrothgar as he mentions the fate of the evil king Heremod: ". . . he departed lonely from the joys of men, the great prince."

We remember in the introduction that "by deeds of praise shall a man flourish in every tribe." It is only fame that will persist after one has departed from this earth, and we are reminded of Beowulf's philosophical statement in Canto XXI: "We each must await an end of our life on earth: let him who is able perform great deeds before death; that will be the best for the warrior when he no longer has life." It is, therefore, wise to consider the ultimate fate of someone who disregards the fame of good deeds and surrenders, as did Heremod, to the promptings of pride.

CANTO XXV

As the sermon on pride continues, Hrothgar mentions the arrogance of an evildoer, an arrogance that grows until the person loses his or her protection against the commands of a cursed spirit. A person like this forgets the future because he or she has been given so many glories in the present. Hrothgar advises Beowulf to avoid these pitfalls and to choose better, eternal counsels. Hrothgar gives thanks to God for the death of the monsters and invites Beowulf to join the renewed feasting. Eager to return home, Beowulf and his followers retire early. Arising early the next morning, Beowulf returns Hrunting to Unferth and gives him his thanks, not mentioning that Hrunting was useless against the monster. This, the poet mentions, is the mark of a great and generous warrior. Finally, Beowulf and his company are ready to depart.

COMMENT

Hrothgar's sermon on pride and arrogance resounds with the biblical admonitions to do good and to beware of the hardening of the heart. Evil, in Hrothgar's sermon, is regarded as a living force that, if not guarded against, may take hold of the spirit. The force of evil is clearly likened to Beowulf's struggle against Grendel and his mother, and Beowulf is warned against falling into the pitfall of thinking that the victory over evil is ever completely won. Hrothgar points out that death will come to Beowulf as it comes to everyone, and so it will benefit him to think on these things. This, of course, leads us back to remarks on the meaning of life made earlier by Beowulf.

Beowulf behaves very generously to Unferth and does not upbraid him for lending him a weapon that proved useless. Beowulf recognizes the good intention of Unferth in giving him the sword; he also realizes that no sword made by mortals would have slain the monster.

CANTO XXVI

Beowulf thanks Hrothgar for his hospitality and pledges that he always will be ready to render assistance to the Danes should it be needed again. Hrothgar replies that he has never in his life heard a more prudent discourse. He praises Beowulf, stating that Beowulf has brought peace between their peoples and predicting that one day Beowulf will be a great king. Hrothgar distributes gifts and takes sad leave of Beowulf: ". . . around the neck he took him, tears fell from him. . . . " Hrothgar's feelings are evidenced in these moving lines: "The man [Beowulf] was so dear to him that he could not restrain the feeling in his breast; but in his heart, held in the bonds of thought, longing after the dear man flamed against blood." Beowulf and his comrades then depart for their boat.

COMMENT

Hrothgar's leave-taking of Beowulf is one of the most moving passages in all of *Beowulf*. We have seen that Hrothgar regards Beowulf as a son and we are reminded of a poem by William Wordsworth (of the modern era) in which the shepherd Michael takes leave of his own son, Luke: ". . . we both may live / To see a better day . . ." This parallels the line in *Beowulf*: ". . . the grizzly haired prince had hope . . . that they might see each other again . . . in conference." In both poems is the indication that both father and son are lost to each other's sight. Hrothgar has a presentiment that he will not see Beowulf again, and Michael is hoping he will again see Luke.

CANTO XXVII

The proud warriors go down to the shore, where they are familiarly greeted by the coast-guardsman. He does not challenge them but instead remarks that their kinsmen will be very happy to see them when they return. Beowulf presents the coast-guardsman with a sword as a gift; then the warriors embark in their ship, loaded with treasure received from Hrothgar. The treasure is carried to Hygelac, Beowulf's lord. We are informed, in a digression, that the queen of Hygelac is Hygd, daughter of Haereth. Hygd is not a miserly queen and not averse to distributing treasure, unlike the atrocious Thryth, the princess whom nobody but her husband dared look in the face. Offa, of the house of Hemming, put a stop to the executions practiced by Thryth. It is said that she practiced less evil after she was given to this young warrior (Offa) and that eventually she became a wise and just ruler in his court.

COMMENT

The coast-guardman appears at the arrival and departure of Beowulf and his companions. He is a character whose treatment is less human than Hrothgar, or even than Unferth, yet he stands out with other briefly appearing characters (such as Wulfgar). He is more real than, for example, King Heremod, or the Frisian Finn. Wulfgar's appearance gives us a bit of insight into the Danish aristocracy, and the coast-guardsman permits us insight into the character of the Danish common warrior or yeoman.

Since Beowulf is the thane of Hygelac, it is fitting that the treasure be carried to Hygelac and be distributed by him. Hygelac is described as the "dispenser of treasure," but no further mention of him is made in this canto.

A digression upon the character of Hygelac's queen Hygd is made, and a further explanatory digression is made into the character of Thryth, later queen of Offa. Again the modern reader may be taken aback by the seeming lack of unity or the unevenness here. These references, however, are pertinent to the audience that either listened to or read *Beowulf,* in much the same way that references contained in the poetry of Robert Browning or T. S. Eliot would be explicable to the educated modern reader.

CANTO XXVIII

Beowulf is greeted by Hygelac and his queen. Hygelac kindly questions Beowulf about what has befallen him and what adventures he has had. Hygelac confesses that he was afraid something might have happened to Beowulf; he also admits that he prayed that Beowulf might not meet the fearful monsters, rather hoping that the Danes would solve their own problems. Hygelac then gives thanks to God for letting him see Beowulf safe and sound again. Beowulf recounts his achievements very briefly and mentions the gifts distributed to the warriors by Wealhtheow. Beowulf also discusses Hrothgar's attempts to secure the peace.

COMMENT

The fear of Hygelac that Beowulf would not return (or that this was a foolhardy venture) harks back to the intimation in Canto III: "His voyage prudent men somewhat criticized, though he was dear to them." Beowulf recounts his adventures only briefly, and the reader is led to suspect that it is to avoid redundancy that another account of the battles is omitted. Beowulf, however, will dwell at length on his deeds in the subsequent chapters—much to the delight of the Anglo-Saxon audience, for whom these encounters provided the focal point of their attention. In the capacity of political advisor, Beowulf remarks on certain political developments that will be taken up subsequently.

CANTO XXIX

The text—from the end of Canto XXVIII to the beginning of
Canto XXX—has been lost entirely.

CANTO XXX

Beowulf is skeptical that peace can be achieved through the
efforts of Hrothgar to marry his daughter to Ingeld, and the
general remarks continue along this line. Beowulf demonstrates how smoldering passions may be fanned into a great
flame of war and that the memories of old enmities cannot be
buried under even the love of a king for his queen. Beowulf
offers his opinion: "Thus, the Heathobards' affection I do not
value. . . . " Beowulf suddenly takes up his account of the
slaying of Grendel and his mother, faithfully reporting what
we have heard earlier.

COMMENT

Beowulf's remarks on the political conditions are
remarkably perspicacious, and his point of analysis is
largely psychological—that is, arising from his knowledge of people. He characterizes the Heathobards as an
impulsive, warlike race who apparently are unaware of
what is good for them. Beowulf's remarks imply the
subsequent destruction of the kingdom of Hrothgar. That
Beowulf does not care too much for the Heathobards is
fairly obvious.

The recapitulation of Beowulf's struggle may bore the
modern reader, inasmuch as it contains no really new
facts or interpretation. Indeed, it is a simplified version
of exactly what we read earlier. Significantly, at the end
Beowulf remarks that he triumphed over Grendel's
mother because, in his opinion, he was "not yet doomed."
This is yet another indication of the Anglo-Saxon
concern with Fate and God, which they combined in
various admixtures. A positive *wyrd* is the interpretation
given the will of God acting in one's behalf.

CANTO XXXI

Beowulf goes on to describe the gifts he received from Hrothgar. The gifts are brought in and laid before Hygelac, who is one of Beowulf's few near kinsmen. Beowulf presents Hygelac with four matched bay horses and also armor, the poet remarking that this is the way kinsmen ought to behave rather than engaging in dark, subtle plots against one another. It is reported that Beowulf presented Hygd with the necklace given him by Queen Wealhtheow, and we are informed that Hygd wore it ever thereafter. We are also informed that Beowulf's reputation had not been great, that he had been looked down upon by his mead-hall companions. Even Hygelac had not really thought him good for much. Beowulf had never killed a drinking companion while he was drunk; he had preserved his great strength until it could be used at the proper time—that is, on the battlefield or against demons and monsters. King Hygelac now presents Beowulf with a sword, the greatest gift that could be given among the Geats. In addition, Beowulf receives seven thousand hides and a mead-hall.

In succeeding years, the kingdom of Hygelac and his son, Heardred (who are both killed) devolves upon Beowulf, who rules it well for fifty years. Then when Beowulf is old and approaching the end of his life, a fire-breathing dragon begins to make its presence known.

COMMENT

The unevenness of *Beowulf* with respect to time is perfectly obvious in this canto. The death of Hygelac and Heardred and the fifty-year reign of Beowulf are mentioned in a scarce dozen lines as opposed to the several-canto interview between Beowulf and Hygelac.

We are surprised to find that Beowulf was not regarded by the Geats as a great hero and that behind his back (it could not be mentioned publicly since Beowulf was a kinsman of the king) Beowulf was spoken of as a weak and sluggish prince: "For a long time the sons of the Goths did not account him of any good, or (did they consider) the Lord of Hosts would place him on the mead-bench of the worthy. . . . " That is, that it would turn out badly because Beowulf was not of the stature of the great warriors. This view of Beowulf parallels the early career of Scyld Sceafing who, as a youth and young man, was regarded as weak and frail, unfit, and without origin. It is perhaps of similar importance that Beowulf has few near kinsmen.

Beowulf's nobility of mind and bearing are again cited by the poet when Beowulf gives his relatives gifts. We remember Beowulf's generous treatment of Unferth, from whom he had received insults and an impotent sword. The gentleness of Beowulf is clearly identifiable with certain Christian virtues later to become manifest in the "polite knight" of Medieval Romance. Beowulf, "in his cups" (when drunk), never killed a companion and always acted "after judgment" (like the crafty Ulysses) because he was aware of "the ample gift of his very great strength that he was given by God." Beowulf now receives the highest honor among the Geats, to the great shame of those who had talked behind his back and slandered his reputation.

The canto ends with an account of the death of Hygelac at the hands of the Swedes, which looks forward to certain predictions made at the time of Beowulf's death. A condensed version of Beowulf's fifty-year rule is given, and we remember that Hrothgar had ruled for half a century when he was nearing the end of his life. Similarly, Beowulf was "a wise king, an old land-guardian, until a dragon began to hold sway on dark nights." The overtones prepare for the account of Beowulf's last struggle.

CANTO XXXII

The thief who stole the cup from the dragon's hoard did not do so out of maliciousness or greed, but rather from necessity. The guilty man was a runaway serf, suffering the displeasure of his master and in need of shelter. He stumbled upon the dragon's lair by accident and, hoping to appease his master, fled in terror with a jeweled cup. The great treasure hoard of the dragon had remained intact for three centuries. It had been buried there by one of the people's nobles "who there longest wandered, a sad man." The noble hoped for an extension to his earthly days that he might enjoy his treasure a little longer and think back to former times. Finally, the sad old noble died, and a dragon who came to defend the treasure slept undisturbed until the discovery of the stolen cup. When the dragon discovered the theft, he ravaged the lands about with fire and destruction. Hearing of this, Beowulf lapses—somewhat incongruously in terms of his previous presentation—into melancholy.

COMMENT

The fragmentary condition of the manuscript makes portions of this canto somewhat ambiguous, and any definite statements concerning the thief are impossible. The theft was performed under "dire necessity," but that is all that may be said with assurance. Through some occurrence (here the lines are missing in whole or in part) the dragon comes to defend the treasure buried by the sad noble.

The section that treats of the noble is called *The Survivor's Lament* and is one of the finest examples of elegiac verse in Old English literature. The passing glories of the earth (his treasure) and his friends and comrades of the sword (whom he will not see again) make the noble sad. His question takes the form of *ubi sunt. . . ?"* (That is, "Where are. . . ?"). (See the remarks on this theme under *The Wanderer,* above.) Perhaps, from the standpoint of Hrothgar's sermon, the noble had not thought about the end of life and had not accepted eternal counsels, preferring instead material glories of the earth. The treasure, he does not realize, could make him little other than sad. Perhaps, as some critics believe, a Christian moral of the vanities of the world is interwoven here. In any case, the noble is tragically involved in his contemplation of treasure that can bring him neither Christian bliss nor Anglo-Saxon fame (*lof,* which for a warrior is best to obtain).

When Beowulf hears of the dragon's outrages, he becomes very melancholy: ". . . his breast boiled within with dark thoughts as was not characteristic of him . . . ." This unexpected reaction on the part of Beowulf is the same as Hrothgar's when his kingdom is threatened by Grendel. Beowulf believes that he has in some way offended against God, and he dwells on this subject to the point of brooding. It is a sharply drawn distinction to the youthful Beowulf!

CANTO XXXIII

When, however, the dragon destroys Beowulf's own home, he vows revenge, as if only this deed could awaken him from his melancholic slumbers. We remember that Beowulf said that to avenge was better than to mourn. Preparing to battle the dragon, Beowulf orders an iron shield to be fashioned. (It is an iron shield rather than a conventional wooden one, which would be of no avail against the dragon's fulminations). The previous deeds of Beowulf are mentioned: his struggle against Grendel and his escape from the Battle of Friesland by swimming with thirty sets of armor on his back. It is mentioned also that Beowulf refused the offer of Hygelac's kingdom, preferring to act as an advisor to youthful Heardred until he came of age. When Heardred was killed by rovers who had overcome the king to the Scylfings, Beowulf accepted the throne.

COMMENT

Beowulf's immediate reaction to the news of the dragon clearly presents the old Beowulf, in contrast to the youthful hero seen earlier. It is only after he personally suffers injury at the hands of the dragon that the heroic spark ignites his will to action. Beowulf vows revenge: "For this [action] the warlike king, the Weders' prince learned vengeance." The poet labors to show that the older Beowulf is still the same hero as of "days of yore," by recounting feats performed by the hero. Still, Beowulf's prowess has clearly diminished through the passage of time, and we are impressed with the notion that this is to be Beowulf's last encounter.

In Beowulf's three struggles, the opposing monsters become less and less personal, less liable to human apprehension. Proceeding from Beowulf's hand-to-hand struggle with Grendel, through his Aeneas-like descent into the underworld, and to his present encounter with the fabulous fire-breathing dragon, Beowulf's powers are lessened or translated into aspects of a superhuman, miraculous agency of Good or Hero. It has been suggested by some critics that the dragon represents a civil war that took place among the Geats; if that is the case (and is so understood by the audience), then the melancholy of the generous Beowulf may be understood.

CANTO XXXIV

Mention is made of Beowulf's friendship to Eadgils, a Swedish prince to whose aid he came earlier in his life. It is stated that Beowulf had outlived every conflict and every enmity. With twelve companions, and guided by the thief who had stolen the cup, Beowulf goes forth to meet the dragon. The thief goes against his will and with a sad mind because he is aware that he provoked the troubles originally, but only he knows the way to the dragon's lair. Beowulf and his companions sit not far from the cave, and Beowulf becomes momentarily saddened because he knows that his end is near: ". . . his mind was sad, wandering and death dwelling, his doom near at hand which the old man must salute and seek his soul-reward, parting asunder life from body. . . . " Although Beowulf is aware that his end is near, he does not despair; instead, he passes through a momentarily lethargic sadness that almost paralyzes his action.

As Beowulf pauses to say farewell to his friends, his mind turns on melancholy topics. Beowulf speaks of his youth and the accidental death of Herebald, oldest of the sons of Hrethel, his guardian. Herebald was killed by one of his brother's arrows. This was an inexplicable accident because whatever happened, Herebald must remain unavenged.

COMMENT

It was the custom in Scandinavia for a man of high birth to give his son into the care of a foster-father in order to be educated; thus there is nothing strange or unusual in Beowulf's upbringing by Hrethel. Saddened by the thoughts that his earthly life soon will be over, Beowulf recounts a sad tale from his youth. The accidental murder of Herebald could be punished; but the significance resides in the fact that Hrethel cannot avenge the death of his own son, since that would mean that he would have to raise his hand against his own kin. Beowulf's thoughts turn to other situations where no vengeance could be exacted. It was, of course, a principle of Anglo-Saxon law that no vengeance could be exacted for an executed criminal. These elegiac lines in *Beowulf* are reminiscent of *The Survivor's Lament,* mentioned earlier.

CANTO XXXV

Beowulf is reminded by Hrethel's heartbreak over Herebald of the struggles between the Swedes and Geats after the death of Hrethel. The sons of Ongentheow, a Swedish king, refused to keep the peace; and Beowulf's kinsmen, Haethcyn and Hygelac, exacted vengeance for the Swedish outrages. The fighting led to the death of Haethcyn, King of the Geats, and Hygelac—as mentioned earlier—obtained vengeance for his brother's murder when Ongentheow met his end by the hands of Eofor. Beowulf mentions Daeghrefn, whom he slew in battle without using his sword but by means of his mighty grip. Beowulf now makes his last *beot:* "I have undertaken many battles in may youth; I will seek again conflict as a sagacious guardian of my people and gloriously defeat the atrocious spoiler if he will seek me out from his earth-hall."

Beowulf takes a final farewell and then, "bold beneath his helm," advances to meet the dragon. He strikes the dragon with his sword but to no avail. Further, his iron shield does not afford him the hoped-for protection against the dragon's flames.

COMMENT

Beowulf's boast shows that he is more heroic, less melancholy: "In my youth I engaged in many wars. Old guardian of the people, I shall still seek battle, perform a deed of fame, if the evil-doer will come to me out of the earth-hall."

Beowulf's sword does not avail him against the dragon, even as Hrunting had not availed him against Grendel's mother. The failure of his sword and the lack of protection afforded by his shield indicate that Beowulf's power is limited and deprived of the miraculous: "The shield protected the life of the great prince for less time than he estimated. . . . " It is noted that his sword bit "less strongly" than was necessary, a further suggestion of the waning powers of Beowulf. Apparently he will not be powerful enough to complete his task. The canto closes with Beowulf encompassed by flames and bereaved of all his thanes—save one who is not afraid to come to his aid.

CANTO XXXVI

A young kinsman of Beowulf, Wiglaf, comes to his aid. Wiglaf is the son of Weohstan, a Swedish prince of the house of Aelfhere. As Wiglaf remembers the character and generosity of Beowulf, he remarks to his companions: "I remember that time when we were drinking mead and we promised our lord in the mead-hall that we would repay him who gave us these rings for our war-equipment if he ever required it of us." To Beowulf, Wiglaf delivers a speech that invigorates the old warrior: "Dear Beowulf, perform as well as you said in your youth that you would, that you would not let your greatness sink while you were alive. . . . "

Wiglaf, who can restrain himself no longer, impulsively hurls himself into the flames carrying a sword given him by Onela (an heirloom of Eanmund, whom his father Weohstan had killed in battle). Full of wrath, the dragon falls upon the two warriors and covers them with flames. The flames consume Wiglaf's wooden shield, and he seeks cover under the iron shield of Beowulf. Beowulf's sword, Naegling, fails its user and snaps in the conflict because "it was not granted Beowulf that iron edges might help in battle." For a third and final time the dragon falls upon Beowulf, this time fastening its poisonous fangs into Beowulf's neck.

COMMENT

Wiglaf, the youthful warrior, is following his lord into battle for the first time. That he is a daring and somewhat reckless youth is evidenced by the fact that he alone, of all the companions who journeyed to the cave, dares to brave the terrible dragon. Wiglaf has reminded his companions of their duty (according to *comitatus*), but they do not heed. It is seen that the young Wiglaf is possessed of certain qualities we remember in the youthful Beowulf—that is, concern with right-acting and the call of duty.

CANTO XXXVII

Wiglaf displays the "craft and courage" that he had inherited. He does not pay any attention to his hand, which is scorched by the dragon's fire. Craftily, he does not strike with his sword at the dragon's head but goes, rather, to a lower and more vulnerable place. He strikes with such force that the moment his sword penetrates the dragon's hide the terrible fire begins to abate. Beowulf, regaining command of his senses, takes his dagger and rips open the dragon's belly. Together, lord and thane, they kill the dragon, and, as the poet observes, this is the manner in which men should act. Beowulf, conscious of the effects of the dragon's venom, sits down to await his end. Wiglaf brings him water and listens to Beowulf as he awaits his impending death: "He knew quite well that his moments and joy on earth had passed through." Beowulf passes briefly over his career and its vicissitudes in a final speech and asks Wiglaf to show him the treasure hoard that he might die more tranquilly.

COMMENT

The perfect example of lord-thane relationship, or *comitatus,* is given and approved here by the poet. Wiglaf risks his own life to save the life and honor of his lord. Fittingly, lord and thane together slay the dragon. Unfortunately, this encounter, as we see, spells the end of Beowulf: It is as the hero expected and in obedience to the all-powerful wyrd. Beowulf says that he can rejoice in his life because he did not swear false oaths, defended what was his, and did not pick quarrels; in other words, he lived up to the highest Ethic of the Anglo-Saxons. He is happy also that he cannot be accused of the most heinous of all crimes, the murder of his own kin.

Significantly, Beowulf asks to view the treasure. We suspect that the moral of *The Survivor's Lament* may be lost here, but this is dispelled when it becomes obvious that the treasure is for Beowulf merely the emblem of his act or the "fruits" of it.

CANTO XXXVIII

Wiglaf quickly obeys the command of Beowulf, going into the dragon's cave for the treasure. He takes as much of the spoil as he can carry and returns to Beowulf, whom he finds on the brink of death. Beowulf looks at the trophies and thanks God that he has been able to acquire such treasure for his people before his death. Beowulf gives direction for the construction of his funeral pyre on Hronesness. He then gives Wiglaf his golden ring, helmet, and byrnie and bids him use them well. "You are the last remnant of our race of Waegmundings: destiny has taken all my kinsmen to the Godhead, earls in their valour; I shall follow them." These are the last words of Beowulf.

COMMENT

Although it is understandable that the warrior-spirit has abated in the aged Beowulf, his nobility and generosity have not changed. We remember his remarks to Hrothgar—that it befits a warrior to do great deeds before the day of his death—and Beowulf, at the moment of his own death, gives thanks that he has performed this last great deed for the benefit of his people. The ironic implications of his acquisition will become apparent shortly. The noble motives of Beowulf in viewing the treasure are obvious: He wishes it not for himself, or, perhaps, even as an emblem of his fame, but rather for his people. Beowulf appears here as a patriarchal figure, as "shepherd of his flock."

CANTO XXXIX

Wiglaf laments the death of his hero, lord, and kinsman. The dragon that has killed Beowulf lies nearby, lifeless and still bleeding. Legend says that no hero, however courageous, had ever braved the dragon's blasting breath or laid a finger upon its treasure hoard. Once again, the companions of Beowulf appear, coming out of the wood to where they had fled. Wiglaf rebukes them as cowards who had no courage to come to the aid of Beowulf when they might have saved his life. Death is better than the dishonor that surely will follow them, he says.

COMMENT

The behavior of Beowulf's comrades here (with the exception, of course, of Wiglaf) is a contrast to the behavior of the "kindred band" of comrades that rose to Beowulf's defense against Grendel. We remember that Beowulf's comrades in Heorot leaped to his defense, although they were of no help. Wiglaf accuses Beowulf's thanes of a breach of *comitatus;* for this they shall be deprived of all their land and must suffer exile. When other nobles hear of their cowardice, it seems, death will be preferable to the shame of their dishonor.

CANTO XL

Wiglaf orders that the results of the struggle be made known to those who waited at the sea-cliff fort. The messenger tells them frankly that both Beowulf and the monster have died and that Wiglaf remains a living hero beside the dead. The messenger predicts that the country will be threatened with war when the Franks and Frisians hear of the fall of the hero. According to the messenger, the Franks have been unfavorably disposed since the death of Hygelac; he does not count on the good will of the Swedes, either.

COMMENT

The gloomy predictions of the messenger upon the death of Beowulf hinge upon previously unresolved quarrels. We remember that Wiglaf's sword was taken from a Swedish king by Wiglaf's father and is thus a reminder of an unsettled blood-feud, furnishing the Swedes with an excuse to declare war when Wiglaf assumes the Geat throne. In the sense that Grendel is a harbinger of the disaster that overtakes the Danes, the dragon can be seen as a harbinger of a disaster that subsequently will overtake the Geats. This is certainly confirmed by the messenger's statements, which are ominous portents.

CANTO XLI

The messenger's retrospective account of the struggles between Hygelac's Geats and the Swedes, led by Ongentheow, is continued. Eofor, as mentioned earlier by Beowulf, killed Ongentheow; in so doing, he won a great reward and the hand of Hygelac's daughter. The messenger contends that this feud is the basis of the future struggles of the Geats and Swedes. After listening to the messenger, the entire company rises and goes to view the body of the fallen warrior and the corpse of the slain dragon. No one dares touch the treasure hoard—except a man of God's own choosing, whomever that might be.

COMMENT

Although the reason for the enmity of the Swedes has already been suggested, the messenger suggests other possibly more cogent facts—facts that, as we remember, were stated by Beowulf in Canto XXXV.

CANTO XLII

The dragon had wrongfully kept the treasure hoard sealed in the barrow. The princes who placed the treasure in the barrow had pronounced a curse on it that should last until the last day of the world. Wiglaf gives the order that lumber be prepared for Beowulf's funeral pyre. Next he summons seven of the best men and with them enters the dragon's cave. After heaving the dragon over the cliff, they pillage the cave and load the gold onto a wagon.

COMMENT

The introductory remarks concern the evils of hoarding and then touch upon the uncertainty of life, a theme that has pervaded *Beowulf* almost from the beginning. The indications of the end of Beowulf—his funeral—become manifest when Wiglaf orders that wood be brought for the funeral pyre.

CANTO XLIII

The Geats prepare a great funeral pyre for Beowulf, as he had asked them to do. The pyre is hung about with helmets, shields, and byrnies. The mourning soldiers lay Beowulf in the midst, and a great funeral fire is lit. The roaring of the flames mingles with the cries of the mourners until the flames subside and the body of the hero crumbles to pieces. Upon the headland a great mound is built in ten days to be seen by seafarers. The cursed treasure is placed in the barrow, as useless now as it was before. The twelve chieftains, all sons of princes, lament their loss as they ride around the barrow. Beowulf is given a final eulogy: "Thus deplored the Geats the fall of their lord; his hearth-enjoyers said that he was of the family of man mildest, and kindest and to his people the gentlest and of praise most desirous."

COMMENT

Thus the epic of *Beowulf* returns to a funeral scene, which is almost where it had begun. The grandeur of Beowulf's funeral is equal to the funeral of the mythical Scyld Sceafing, mentioned in the first chapter. Ironically, the treasure, which Beowulf wished to win for his people, is useless to everyone. This is the final irony of *Beowulf,* dealing as it does with the illusion and uncertainty of life against which a hero must strive.

INDEX OF CHARACTERS

Aelfhere: Ancestor of Weohstan and Wiglaf.

Aeschere: Elder brother of Yrmenlaf; Hrothgar's "dear friend," who is killed by Grendel's mother.

Beanstan: Father of Breca.

Beowulf: There are two Beowulfs in the epic. The first is the son of Scyld Sceafing and the grandfather of Hrothgar. The other Beowulf, the hero of the poem, is the son of Ecgtheow and nephew of Hygelac. The first Beowulf is a Dane; the second, a Geat.

Breca: Son of Beanstan and king of the Brondings, with whom, as a young man, Beowulf had his famous swimming contest.

Daeghrefn: Champion of the Franks who was killed by Beowulf with his "grip of iron," when Hygelac invaded the Netherlands and Rhine valley.

Eadgils: A Swedish prince, son of Ohthere and brother of Eanmund. Beowulf came to his assistance when he invaded Sweden.

Eanmund: Brother of Eagdils; killed by Weohstan, father of Wiglaf.

Ecglaf: Father of Unferth.

Ecgtheow: Father of Beowulf the Geat; he married the daughter of Hrethel, father of Hygelac.

Eofor: Son of Wonred and brother of Wulf; killed the Swedish king Ongentheow.

Eomer: Son of Offa.

Eormenric: Historical king of Ostrogoths.

Finn: King of the Frisians and also ruler of the Jutes; son of Folcwanda and husband of Hildeburh, sister of Hnaef. In a war with Hnaef's Danes, Finn is killed. (See *The Fight at Finnsburg*)

Fitela: Son, nephew, and companion of Sigemund.

Folcwanda: Father of Finn.

Freawaru: Daughter of Hrothgar; married Ingeld, prince of Heathobards.

Froda: King of the Heathobards and father of Ingeld.

Garmund: Father of Offa.

Grendel: Monster who ravaged Heorot. He descended from Cain.

Guthlaf: A Dane, one of Hnaef's and Hengest's followers.

Haereth: Father of Hygd, wife of Hygelac.

Haethcyn: Son of Hrethel; killed his brother Herebald by accident. Ongentheow, the Swedish king, later killed him.

Halga: Son of Danish king Healfdene, brother of Hrothgar and Heorogar.

Hama: Germanic mythical hero.

Healfdene: Danish king, son of Beowulf the Dane, father of Hrothgar, Heorogar, and Halga.

Heardred: Son of Hygelac and later king of Geats; killed by Swedish king Onela and succeeded by Beowulf the Geat.

Heatholaf: Wylfing killed by Ecgtheow.

Hengest: Danish chief; assumed command of Danes after Hnaef's death.

Heorogar: Son of Healfdene, brother of Hrothgar and Halga, father of Heoroweard.

Heoroweard: Son of Danish king Heorogar; nephew of Hrothgar.

Herebald: Geat prince, son of Hrethel; accidentally killed by his brother Haethcyn.

Heremod: Danish king specifically cited as the negative example of a ruler.

Hildeburh: Danish princess, daughter of Hoc and wife of Finn; sister of Hnaef, king of Danes.

Hnaef: King of the Danes, killed by Finn's men.

Hoc: The father of Hildeburh.

Hondscio: One of Beowulf's followers, killed by Grendel in Heorot.

Hrethel: Geat king, father of Hygelac and Haethcyn, grandfather of Beowulf.

Hrethric: Son of Hrothgar; later killed by Hrothulf.

Hrothgar: King of the Danes; son of Healfdene; brother of Heorogar and Halga; husband of Wealhtheow; father of Hrethric, Hrothmund, and Freawaru.

Hrothmund: Son of Hrothgar.

Hrothulf: Nephew of Hrothgar; son of Hrothgar's brother, Halga.

Hunlafing: Danish follower of Hnaef.

Hygd: Wife of Hygelac; daugther of Haereth; mother of Heardred. Her name means "prudence."

Hygelac: Beowulf's uncle and lord; king of the Geats; husband of Hygd; father of Heardred.

Ingeld: Prince of unruly Heathobards; son of Froda; married to Freawaru (daughter of Hrothgar). Beowulf does not believe that this political alliance will keep the peace.

Offa: King of the Angles; husband of Thryth.

Ohthere: Son of Ongentheow; brother of Onela; father of Eanmund and Beowulf's friend, Eadgils.

Onela: Swedish king; son of Ongentheow; he killed the Geatish king Heardred; later killed by his nephew.

Ongentheow: Swedish king; father of Onela and Ohthere; killer of the Geat king Haethcyn; killed by Eofor.

Oslaf: A Danish follower of Hnaef and Hengest.

Scyld Sceafing: Mythological founder of the Danish royal house. His name literally means "child with sheaf."

Sigemund: Legendary Germanic hero; son of Waels. The story of Sigemund is sung in *Beowulf*.

Thryth: Wife of Offa.

Unferth: Hrothgar's *thyle* (spokesman); son of Ecglaf; he taunts Beowulf, who refers to Unferth's alleged murder of his brothers; he comes to respect Beowulf and lends him his sword, Hrunting, for the underwater battle with Grendel's mother.

Waels: Father of Sigemund.

Wealhtheow: Wife of Hrothgar; called the "peacemaker," and the "Dane's Damsel." The only female figure in *Beowulf* to assume any sort of identity of her own.

Weohstan: Father of Wiglaf; killer of Eanmund, brother of Eagdils who was later to become king of Sweden. The implications of a blood-feud are obvious and mentioned indirectly by the messenger who announces Beowulf's death.

Wiglaf: Son of Weohstan; comes to Beowulf's aid during fight with dragon; subsequent ruler of the Geats.

Wonred: Father of Eofor and Wulf.

Wulf: Son of Wonred and brother of Eofor.

Wulfgar: Chief of the Wendels and advisor at the court of Hrothgar.

Yrmenlaf: Brother of Aeschere (Hrothgar's friend).

ESSAY QUESTIONS AND ANSWERS

QUESTION

In your opinion, are the historical digressions (for example, *The Fight at Finnsburg*) in *Beowulf* conducive to the "unity" of the epic? Explain.

ANSWER

In terms of modern criticism, the digressions of Beowulf are sometimes not considered conducive to the unity of the poem because they are occasionally repetitious (as the account of Eofor's struggle with Ongentheow) or seem to pertain little to the matter at hand (for example, the account given of Thryth, wife of Offa, when Hygd is the subject under discussion). Modern scholars, however, have demonstrated that many of the digressions were exceedingly appropriate for the Anglo-Saxon audience to which they were addressed. These digressions served to unify *Beowulf* with a common body of tradition and with facts that were certainly well known to an educated audience. This may be likened to our appreciation of Leo Tolstoy's *War and Peace* from our familiarization with the facts of the Napoleonic Wars. Also, these digressions formed part of the poet's technique. By mention of certain historical facts, the poet is able at times to introduce irony into the work. An example would be in the description of Hrothgar's wondrous hall, Heorot, which "unfriendly fire awaits." This clearly refers to a future time when Hrothgar's kingdom will be invaded. In addition, some critics have shown that the heroic elements of these fragments offer meaningful parables with the life and character of Beowulf.

QUESTION

How would you resolve the apparent contradiction between the elements of Christian faith and Teutonic myth that appear in *Beowulf*?

ANSWER

Historically the intermingling of Christian and Teutonic elements in *Beowulf* occurs because this intermingling of beliefs was also true of Anglo-Saxon society at this time. The conversion of the Anglo-Saxons did not take place until little more than a century before the composition of *Beowulf,* and it is easy to see that the Germanic traditions could not be—and were not, according to the policy of the Roman Church—stamped out immediately.

QUESTION

Why does Wiglaf decree that those who deserted Beowulf when he went to meet the dragon would suffer exile and loss of their lands? Explain in terms of Anglo-Saxon custom.

ANSWER

The warriors who deserted their lord on the battlefield were guilty of violating the lord-thane relationship. This relationship, an old Germanic custom—called *comitatus* by Tacitus—provided that young men attach themselves to some mature warrior. Their obligation was to provide the lord with their services on the battlefield. The obligation of the lord was to provide protection for each thane and a share of all bounty or treasure. It was considered an extreme dishonor for a thane to leave the battlefield before his lord—and an extreme dishonor for the lord if he did not excel all his thanes in valor. This institution, which is similar to the later feudal institution, was of extreme importance to the Anglo-Saxons. Wiglaf, we remember, remarks that "death is better than such dishonor," that is, violation of *comitatus.*

QUESTION

Explain the meaning and function of kenning.

ANSWER

The kenning is a poetical device whereby a figurative phrase is substituted for a direct reference to the object itself, such as "battle-flasher" for "sword" and "whale-road" for "sea." Kenning tends to be an exaggeration of the poetic tendency to synthesize experience but does not necessarily restrict itself to less sophisticated poetry. Examples of kenning (in the form of euphuism) persist in the lyrics of the eighteenth-century English Augustans, such as in Pope's use of "finny breed" for "fish." The peculiar circumstance that rendered kenning so common in *Beowulf* is the four-beat alliterative line, which was very strictly adhered to as part of the scop's tradition. Such restrictions on the flow of language naturally resulted in the substitution of two-beat phrases in the form of kennings for ordinary words that would not fit into the line.

QUESTION
Relate *Beowulf* to the conventional idea of the "epic."

ANSWER:
There is no single quality that defines an epic, and all epics have distinctive qualities. Usually epics are divided into primary and secondary. *Beowulf* is a primary epic in that it is not (as far as we know) modeled after classical examples like the *Iliad*. It arose out of an oral tradition, like the *Iliad,* and is not literary in origin. *Beowulf* is considered an epic on the grounds that it was written in an exalted, dignified style; that it has a complex theme and narrative that recapitulate the significant preoccupations and experiences of the heroic epoch in Anglo-Saxon tradition; that it presents a hero who is the epitome of a nation and culture; and that it links the heroic deeds of the hero with the whole history and tradition of a people. Beowulf is the focal point of the whole work, as Achilles is the focal point of the *Iliad*. The poet concentrates on a specific section of the hero's life (or on two sections, unified in theme and quality). And we see *Beowulf* in relation to the history of the important peoples: Scyld Sceafing and the Scyldings, the struggle between the Danes and the Heathobards, and so on. Furthermore, the style (the epic "high style") of the work is elaborate and rhetorical in a way that embodies the spirit of its heroic subject.

QUESTION

Describe the characteristics and function of a scop.

ANSWER

Early written literatures are almost always the product of a long oral tradition that developed out of songs and spoken poems. In the case of Anglo-Saxon literature, the oral tradition goes back to the Germanic tribes that inhabited the Continent. The scop (literally, "shaper") was a poet-singer who wandered to various courts in search of a patron among the lords. The scop was to entertain during feasts, singing lyrical or heroical poems. He sang of real and legendary heroes whose names lived on because of the song. In *Beowulf* a scop sings at Hrothgar's court about Sigemund (the Volsung) and his heroic defeat of the dragon. But the subject matter of the scop—at least the subject matter that has survived in the manuscripts (dating from around A.D. 1000)—became influenced by Christian notions and adapted traditions of the heroic age according to Christian interpretations.

QUESTION

Is it likely that the *Beowulf* poet looked to contemporary events for subject matter and general inspiration? If so, would you consider the poem a sort of social criticism in the sense, say, of the plays of Shaw?

ANSWER

Most scholars agree that the *Beowulf* legend comes out of a period long before the date of the poem's composition. The poem makes use of a heroic tradition that came down to the poet and his audience through a long oral tradition. Of course it is possible that the legend is based upon real historical events, but whatever actuality stands behind the poem has clearly been embellished in a way clearly separated from historical events. The story of Beowulf is mythical in much the sense that the Tale of Troy is mythical in its uses by Homer and, for that matter, the fourteenth century Chaucer in *Troilus and Criseyda.* The *Beowulf* poet was concerned with finding a significant story—one that would embody and render meaningful the elements of the audience and himself in a way that made poetry or "song." As Lord Raglan argues in *The Hero,* a people, especially at the time of *Beowulf,* can completely forget their actual past within a century and a half. This fact seems partially to explain the tendency of poets to turn to myth, for it remains long after historical facts have faded. As Professor Gilbert Murray argues in *The Rise of the Greek Epic, Beowulf* is like the Homeric poems in that neither refers to specific warfare or other "heroic" events in their recent history. He concluded that this seems "to be the natural tendency of a poet, at least of an epic poet."

There remains the question of the function of the poem in terms of the society: Does it amount to "social criticism"? There has been little general agreement among readers on this point. On one hand, there seems to be an establishment of heroic values that could serve almost as doctrine to the audience of the poet, as we have seen in *The Wanderer:* "A councilor must be patient, / not too impetuous nor too hasty of speech / not too weak in war nor too reckless / nor too timid nor too venturesome nor too greedy / nor ever too ready to make boasts before he understands them." On the other hand, *Beowulf* was a sort of song (or perhaps symphony is closer to the fact) that the wandering poet or scop sang (probably to a harp like the one found in Sutton Hoo) in order to entertain his audience. It is highly unlikely that the poet saw himself as a social reformer in the sense of a Shaw; for whereas Shaw dramatized ideas designed to bring society some sort of salvation, *Beowulf* is an epic recapitulation of the significant ideals and progress of a people, and it is a poem.

QUESTION
What contribution has *Beowulf* made to our understanding of the early civilization in England? Is it possible to draw specific conclusions about the customs and ways of life from the poem alone?

ANSWER

Our knowledge of Anglo-Saxon civilization has been an inter-pretation based on historical records and the literature of the time. For many years historians and anthropologists and literary scholars (the only readers of *Beowulf* until quite recently) conjectured and arrived at strikingly different views of Old English life. For example, was the famous burial scene in *Beowulf* a true description of the elaborate rites of the time (or an earlier time), or was it a fantastic invention by the poet to embellish a historical past and thereby glorify the nation? It is probably true, as some critics have argued, that *Beowulf* is a patriotic poem, designed to exalt the virtues and achievements of the people. But this does not prevent some of the detail—perhaps a great deal of it—from being accurate transcription of life of the past (the poet's past, rather than his contemporary civilization).

Archaeological discoveries, especially Sutton Hoo, have led us to believe that detailed descriptions such as that of the burial in the poem are not fantastic after all. The burial-ship found at Sutton Hoo contained extraordinary riches, and the articles, as Prof. Wrenn and others have shown, contribute to our understanding of the poem and its relation to the civilization. Before *Beowulf,* the only extensive written record we have of the Germanic peoples is Tacitus's *Germania,* completed in A.D. 97–98. *Beowulf* confirms a good deal of what Tacitus said. An example of this is what Tacitus called the *comitatus*—the relationship of the warrior to his lord, instances of which abound in the poem. We recall that, at the end of *Beowulf,* when the hero is deserted by his followers (except for the noble Wiglaf) and left to die in battle, Wiglaf curses them and tells them that because of their violation of a sacred relationship, their wealth and land is forfeit. Wiglaf notes that a warrior's death is highly preferable to the dishonorable one they now will endure. In a sense, therefore, *Beowulf* represents a dramatic version of many of the ideals and aspirations of the people.

We note that the dramatis personae of the poem are warriors and their enemies, not the common people of the time. In this respect, the poem gives us only a partial picture of the civilization—that is, the noble, controlling element of the society. But we are given an understanding of feudalism—with its highly stratified social relationships and its implications for the whole society. We also are given a background for understanding, for the first time, the confrontation of Roman law and classical civilization with feudalism—a way of life that could not lend itself to the Roman ideals, such as the divine right of kings. Furthermore, *Beowulf* gives us many details of the customs that do not immediately seem relevant, such as (in the words of Professor Chadwick in *The Heroic Age,* Cambridge, 1912, p. 82) "the long detailed account of Beowulf's arrival at the Danish king's hall, and the conversation which the chamberlain holds with the king on the one hand and the visitor on the other, before the latter is invited to enter." This custom of keeping someone standing at the door is related by Lord Raglan, in *The Hero,* to ritual drama (which he holds to be the source of myths, as opposed to historical events as the source of myths). In ritual drama the setting is very often a doorway (or a gateway). Lord Raglan concludes (*The Hero,* Vintage Books, 1956, p. 255): "The reason for this is probably that the ritual was originally performed at the king's palace or tomb, which was often the same place." This example from *Beowulf* and from conclusions drawn from it demonstrates another way in which the poem aids our understanding of early civilization and the myths and literature they produced. Thus we do learn a great deal about the people from the poem, but our knowledge becomes complete—if it ever does— only as we combine our findings with the discoveries of history and of literatures in general.

CRITICAL COMMENTARY

There are many views on the complex poems of Anglo-Saxon literature. *Beowulf* is our only native epic, but that is not our reason for studying it. For centuries it was forgotten; and even when it was published and studied in the nineteenth century, it was considered the product of a barbarous age at best. Critical opinion has raised the reputation of *Beowulf* and other Old English poems a great deal in our time. Anglo-Saxons of the time of the Beowulf-poet were a sophisticated people who had developed a complex literature that includes a number of poems ranking with the greatest works in the language. Below we shall consider some important critical statements on *Beowulf*.

ANTHOLOGY OF CRITICAL VIEWS

Some of the best critical articles on *Beowulf* have been collected in *An Anthology of Beowulf Criticism,* edited by Lewis E. Nicholson (University of Notre Dame Press, 1963, paperback). Briefly, these are the views:

1. Paull F. Baum, "The *Beowulf* Poet." Baum examines the role of the poet behind *Beowulf,* focusing on the demands that the poem must have made upon its audience. The poet "adopted a tense crowded style and a convoluted method of narration, the very antithesis of a minstrel's, most unsuited for recitation, and if he looked for an audience of listeners he was extraordinarily, not to say stubbornly, sanguine." The portrait is one of a highly individualistic poet—not the stereotype one usually imagines as the person of a minstrel or scop.

The other articles in the collection include D. W. Robertson, Jr., "The Doctrine of Charity in Medieval Literary Gardens: A Topical Approach Through Symbolism and Allegory"; Allen Cabaniss, "*Beowulf* and the Liturgy"; and M. B. McNamee, Society of Jesus, "*Beowulf*—An Allegory of Salvation?"

2. F. A. Blackburn, "The Christian Coloring of *Beowulf.*" This essay appeared in 1897 and presented the view—typical among critics of the time—of the poem as having no poetic value. The Christian element was seen as the "coloring" by a later editor, something acquired later than the original creation. The essay concerned itself (like the one by Chadwick, which follows) more with the origins of the poem than with the text itself. Blackburn and Chadwick see the *Beowulf*-poet as a heathen whose work fell later into the hands of a Christian minstrel or scribe who wished to make it Christian. This led to what are held to be inconsistencies in the text.

3. Morton Bloomfield, "*Beowulf* and Christian Allegory: An Interpretation of Unferth." Bloomfield argues that the character of Unferth (which has received more and more attention as a significant figure in the poem) is intended to have allegorical significance as a personification of the abstraction of Discordia. This conclusion is drawn on the basis of a comparison with the allegorical method in Christian Latin poetry. Bloomfield points out that this interpretation is in keeping with the statements of Schücking (mentioned below) on the ideal of kingship based on the Augustinian conception of the perfect ruler. For other articles on the importance of Unferth in *Beowulf,* see James L. Rosier, "Design for Treachery: The Unferth Intrigue," *Publications of the Modern Language Association of America* (*PMLA*), LXXVI (March 1962), pp. 1–7. Rosier sees the Unferth design for treachery as of equal importance with the Grendel episode. "Grendel and his mother pose an external threat to the stability of the hall [Heorot], whereas Hrothulf and Unferth represent an internal menace." He sees several points of likeness between Unferth and Grendel. Rosier agrees basically with the Bloomfield interpretation cited above, though he sees the Christian/allegorical view as "unnecessary, if not unjust to the more literal but dramatic design of the poet." For an answer to the Rosier interpretation, see J. D. A. Ogilvy, "Unferth: Foil to Beowulf?", *PMLA,* LXXIX (September 1964), pp. 350–375. Ogilvy suggests

possibilities other than those in Rosier, implying that Unferth is not so evil as we may assume. (Much of the debate rests on the reading of the title given to Unferth: *thyle,* which usually is defined as spokesman or orator, but is redefined by Rosier as being a pejorative title).

Unferth is acquitted of much of his wickedness by another critic: Norman E. Eliason, "The *thyle* and *Scop* in *Beowulf,*" *Speculum,* XXXVIII (1963), pp. 267–284. Note that Bloomfield has another article in this book, "Patristics and Old English Literature," which demonstrates the significance of the Latin fathers in Old English literature.

4. H. Munro Chadwick. *The Homeric Age,* an excerpt. Chadwick (mentioned above), on the basis of studies of some seventy Christian passages in *Beowulf,* argues that the heathen poet knew very little about Christianity.

5. Margaret E. Goldsmith, "The Christian Perspective in *Beowulf.*" Goldsmith is not in agreement with Rogers' attack on the failure of the poet to impose his moral ideas on his source, saying: "if a martial epic of *Beowulf* was known to our poet, he has taken pains to recast it in quite another mold." She sees the war-descriptions, banquets, and swimming feats as the poet's way of expressing the eternal aspects (largely the moral aspects) of existence.

6. Marie Padgett Hamilton, "The Religious Principle in *Beowulf.*" Hamilton argues that the poet reinterprets his own Germanic background in light of the Christian (Augustinian) view of history.

7. R. E. Kaske, "S*apienta et Fortitudo* as the Controlling Theme of *Beowulf.*" An examination of the themes of wisdom and strength, showing the fusion of Germanic and Christian concepts. The article argues that the poem is thematically unified.

8. Francis P. Magoun, Jr., "The Oral Formulaic Character of Anglo-Saxon Poetry." This important, controversial study has led to a new school of Anglo-Saxon literary criticism. Magoun analyzes lines 1–25 of *Beowulf* and lines 512–535 of Christ and Satan to show the oral formulaic patterns in the poetry.

9. Kemp Malone, "*Beowulf.*" He sees a unity in the two parts of the poem through the poet's patriotism for "Germania" and the spiritual quality of *Beowulf.* The poet himself is a patriotic Englishman. Malone analyzes the poem in terms of its episodes, rather than its general plot.

10. H. L. Rogers, "Beowulf's Three Great Fights." Rogers does not disagree with Tolkien (below) about the theme of the poem, but he believes that the poem is not an artistic unity due to the poet's inability to impose his moral ideas on his source. The poem is not, as Tolkien suggests, an "opposition of ends and beginnings" but a progression in Beowulf's three major fights. Rogers examines the motifs of weapons, treasure, and society in the poem, and he sees the second and third fights as less successful artistically than the first.

11. Levin L. Schücking, "The Ideal of Kingship in *Beowulf.*" Schücking, like Hamilton (above), holds a view contrary to those mentioned of Blackburn and Chadwick. The *Beowulf*-poet is seen as a Christian reshaper of heathen Germanic traditions of the warrior-ethic that runs through the poem. The ideal of kingship is defined largely in terms of the writings of the Church: the "rex justus" (just king) of Augustine.

12. J. R. R. Tolkien, *Beowulf,* "The Monsters and the Critics." Tolkien's essay represents the beginning of the new criticism of *Beowulf,* for it challenges the previously held view that the poem had little organic unity—little structure—and was held together only through the character of the central hero. The monsters in the poem represent evil and chaos and are therefore the center of the action, but the real subject is the tragedy

of the human condition. He sees a symbolic unity in the poem, a rise and fall, "a balance of ends and beginnings" and "the moving contrast of youth and age."

13. C. L. Wrenn, "Sutton Hoo and *Beowulf.*" Prof. Wrenn systematically examines the evidence of the archaeological discovery of Sutton Hoo (the standard, the shield, the helmet, and the musical instrument), showing that the findings were ritually significant and that they are helpful in our study of *Beowulf.* For further information on Sutton Hoo, see Roger H. Hodgkin, *A History of the Anglo-Saxons* (3rd ed., London: Oxford University Press, 1953), II, pp. 696–734: the authoritative survey of the Sutton Hoo ship in Bruce-Mitford's Appendix. Also, on the importance of the harp in reading Old English poetry, see J. B. Bessinger, "*Beowulf* and the Harp at Sutton Hoo," *University of Toronto Quarterly* (January 1958).

14. Herbert G. Wright, "Good and Evil; Light and Darkness; Joy and Sorrow in *Beowulf.*" Wright defends the unity of *Beowulf* on purely textual grounds (unlike many critics, such as those mentioned above who argue from evidence of social and literary history and from biblical exegesis). He sees the poem's unity as being accomplished through an interrelation of imagery of opposites: light and darkness, which are concrete effects related to good and evil, joy and sorrow. (This essay calls into question the view of some critics who hold that the analysis of the poem as a unity is oversubtle; such a view is presented by T. M. Gang, "Approaches to *Beowulf,*" *Review of English Studies,* New Series III (1952), pp. 1-12.)

BIBLIOGRAPHY

BOOK-LENGTH STUDIES OF BEOWULF

Among the important books on *Beowulf* are the following:

1. Peter S. Baker, ed., *Beowulf: Basic Readings,* New York, 1995. A collection of the best critical essays about *Beowulf* published between 1966 and 1990, plus two essays new to this volume.

2. Arthur G. Brodeur, *The Art of Beowulf,* Berkeley, 1959. An important study which, except for the chapter on Diction, can be read without a knowledge of Old English. Among the points of study are Variation, Structure and Unity, Christian and Pagan, and Episodes and Digressions.

3. George Clark, *Beowulf,* Boston, 1990. Part of the Twayne English Authors series.

4. Raymond W. Chambers, *Beowulf: An Introduction to the Study of the Poem with a Discussion of the Stories of Offa and Finn;* 3rd ed., revised by Charles L. Wrenn, Cambridge, Mass., 1959. An important work for advanced students; it has an extensive bibliography.

5. James Whitby Earl, *Thinking About Beowulf,* Stanford, 1994. A psychological study, with special emphasis on concepts of free will and determinism in *Beowulf.*

6. R. D. Fulk, ed., *Interpretations of Beowulf: A Critical Anthology,* Bloomington, 1991. A collection of analytical literary essays.

7. Gwyn Jones, *Kings, Beasts and Heroes,* London, 1972. A study that focuses on the major characterizations of this epic.

8. William W. Lawrence, *Beowulf and Epic Tradition,* Cambridge, Mass., 1928. A highly scholarly study of the epic elements brought together in the poem.

9. J. D. A. Ogilvy and Donald C. Baker, *Reading Beowulf: An Introduction to the Poem, Its Background, and Its Style,* Norman, Okla., 1983. A good overview for the student first getting to know Beowulf.

ARTICLES ON BEOWULF

The student of *Beowulf* should consult the *PMLA* and other cumulative indexes in the library for articles on *Beowulf.* Here is a partial list of important statements on the structure and unity of the poem:

1. Joan Bloomfield, "The Style and Structure of *Beowulf,*" *Review of English Studies,* XIV (1938), 396–403.

2. Adrien Bonjour, The Digressions in *Beowulf, Medium Aevum* Monographs, V, Oxford, 1950.

3. Arthur G. Brodeur, "The Structure and Unity of *Beowulf,*" *PMLA,* LXVIII (1953), 1183–1195.

4. Arthur E. Du Bois, "The Unity of *Beowulf,*" *PMLA,* XLIX (1934), 374–405.

5. Peter F. Fisher, "The Trials of the Epic Hero in *Beowulf,*" *PMLA,* LXXIII (1958), 171–183.

6. Clare Kinney, "The Needs of the Moment: Poetic Foregrounding as a Narrative Device in *Beowulf,*" *Studies in Philology,* LXXXII (1985), 295–314.

7. J. L. N. O'Loughlin, "*Beowulf*—Its Unity and Purpose," *Medium Aevum,* Monographs XXI (1952), 1–13.

8. Peter Richardson, "Imperfective Aspect and Episodic Structure in *Beowulf*," *Journal of English and Germanic Philology,* XCIII (1994), 313-325.

ON SPECIFIC ASPECTS OF BEOWULF

1. Lenore Abraham, "The Decorum of *Beowulf*," *Philological Quarterly,* LXXII (1993), 267–287.

2. Robert A. Albano, "The Role of Women in Anglo-Saxon Culture: Hildeburh in *Beowulf* and a Curious Counterpart in the *Volsunga Saga*," *English Language Notes,* XXXII (1994), 1–10.

3. Theodore M. Andersson, "The Thief in *Beowulf*," *Speculum,* LIX (1984), 493–508.

4. Robert E. Bjork, "Speech as a Gift in *Beowulf*," *Speculum,* LXIX (1994), 993–1022.

5. Arthur E. Du Bois, "The Dragon in *Beowulf*," *PMLA,* LXXII (1957), 819–822.

6. Linda Georgianna, "King Hrethel's Sorrow and the Limits of Heroic Action in *Beowulf*," *Speculum,* LXII (1987), 829–850.

7. Kent Gould, "*Beowulf* and Folktake Mythology: God as Magical Donor," *Folklore,* XCIX (1985), 98–103.

8. Joseph Harris, "Beowulf's Last Words," *Speculum,* LXVII (1992), 1–32.

9. Norma Kroll, "*Beowulf:* The Hero as Keeper of Human Polity," *Modern Philology,* LXXXIV (1986), 117–129.

10. Joyce Tally Lionarons, "*Beowulf:* Myth and Monsters," *English Studies,* LXII (1996), 1–14.

11. Robert M. Lumiansky, "The Dramatic Audience in *Beowulf*," *Journal of English and Germanic Philology*, LI (1952), 545–550.

12. Ward Parks, "Prey Tell: How Heroes Perceive Monsters in *Beowulf*," *Journal of English and Germanic Philology*, XCII (1993), 1–16.

13. Kenneth Sisam, "Beowulf's Fight with the Dragon," *Review of English Studies*, New Series IX (1958), 129–140.

14. Raymond P. Tripp, "Lifting the Curse on *Beowulf*," *English Language Notes*, XXIII (1985), 1–8.

TRANSLATIONS

There are a number of adequate translations, each one attempting to reconstruct the effect of the poem in a different way. The student should compare at least two translations:

1. R. K. Gordon, *Anglo-Saxon Poetry* (Everyman's Library 794, New York, 1962). Has reliable translations of *Beowulf* and other Old English poetry.

2. Stanley B. Greenfield, *A Readable Beowulf* (Southern Illinois University Press, Carbondale, Ill., 1982). Reading that resembles modern prose.

3. J. R. Clark Hall and C. L. Wrenn, *Beowulf and the Finnesburg Fragment* (London, 1950; rev. ed., 1973). An excellent translation, attempting to recapture some of the character of the original.

4. Edwin Morgan, *Beowulf* (Berkeley, 1962).

5. David Wright, *Beowulf* (Penguin Classics L. 70, New York, 1957). Very readable, in modern prose, with interesting introduction and discussion of the problems of translation.

BILINGUAL EDITION

A good paperback bilingual edition, with the Old and Modern English juxtaposed by the half-line, which will enable the beginning student of Anglo-Saxon to enter rather painlessly into the original text is *Beowulf: A Dual-Language Edition,* translated and with an introduction and commentary by Howell D. Chickering, Jr. (New York: Doubleday, 1977).

IMPORTANT MODERN EDITIONS IN ANGLO-SAXON

1. Fr. Klaeber, *Beowulf and the Fight at Finnesburg,* 3rd ed., Boston, 1936. Supplements 1941, 1950. The preferred edition with extensive notes, introduction, glossary, and annotated bibliography.

2. Charles L. Wrenn, *Beowulf: With the Finnesburg Fragment,* London, 1953; revised and enlarged, 1958. Extremely important edition with highly useful introduction.

OLD ENGLISH GRAMMARS

The student wishing to learn Anglo-Saxon should use one of the following grammars. The reading can be supplemented by listening to the recordings listed below of Old English poetry.

1. Alistair Campbell, *Old English Grammar,* London, 1959. More for the specialist.

2. Constance B. Hieatt, *Essentials of Old English: Readings with Keyed Grammar and Vocabulary,* New York, 1968. A good elementary descriptive grammar.

3. Randolph Quirk and C. L. Wrenn, *An Old English Grammar,* 2nd ed., London, 1958. A clear, easy-to-use grammar with special emphasis on the importance of syntax.

DICTIONARIES

1. Joseph Bosworth, *An Anglo-Saxon Dictionary,* Oxford, 1988 (revision of Bosworth's 1898 edition).

2. J. R. Clark Hall, *A Concise Anglo-Saxon Dictionary,* Cambridge, 1931.

BACKGROUND MATERIAL

Among the many useful books are the following:

1. Peter H. Blair, *An Introduction to Anglo-Saxon England,* (Cambridge, England, 1960). A good introduction for the general reader to political, social, economic, and ecclesiastical history of the period.

2. Peter Clemoes, *Interaction of Thought and Language in Old English Poetry,* (Cambridge, N.Y., 1995). Part of the Cambridge Studies in Anglo-Saxon England series, covering the background of the era and the poetry that arose from it.

3. John M. Hill, *The Cultural World in Beowulf,* (Toronto, 1995). An anthropological study that focuses on Anglo-Saxon and Germanic traditions in literature.

3. Fred C. Robinson, *The Tomb of Beowulf and Other Essays on Old English,* (Cambridge, Mass., 1993). Covers aspects of Old English language and culture, the historical and religious setting of *Beowulf,* and criticism of the best-known Old English poems.

4. David Zesmer, *Guide to English Literature From Beowulf through Chaucer and Medieval Drama,* (College Outline Series No. 53, Barnes and Noble, New York, 1961). An extremely useful introduction with extensive annotated bibliographies.

SPECIAL ARTICLES

Among the articles referred to in this book are the following:

1. James L. Rosier, "The Literal-Figurative Identity of *The Wanderer*," *PMLA*, LXXIX (1964), pp. 366–370. A brilliant analysis of The Wanderer using the principles of generative composition: see explanation in The Elements of Anglo-Saxon Poetry in this guide.

2. C. L. Wrenn, "On the Continuity of English Poetry," *Anglia*, LXXVI (1958), 49–59. Prof. Wrenn argues that there has been a greater continuity in the tradition of English poetry than is usually presumed, especially in metrical patterns and in subject matter, thought, and mood.

RETELLING

In 1972, John Gardner's *Grendel* was published in the United States (by Ballantine Books). This brief novel tells the story of *Beowulf,* through the battle with Grendel, from the monster's point of view. In so doing, it challenges the reader to reexamine the concept of heroism—indeed, the entire world view—presented in the traditional story.

RECORDING

There are a number of recordings of readings of Old English, the best of which is J. B. Bessinger's on Caedmon Records. Prof. Bessinger's readings are alive in a way that gets across the qualities of poetry in Caedmon's *Hymn* (sung with a Sutton Hoo type of harp), *The Wanderer,* parts of *Beowulf, A Dream of the Rood,* and *The Battle of Brunanburh.* The readings demonstrate the complex music which is undoubtedly present, in different ways, in each of the poems. Highly recommended.

NOTES

NOTES

NOTES

NOTES

NOTES

NOTES

NOTES